Among Friends

Inspiring And Impactful Stories From the Soul

Written By

Edna L. Isaac

Alongside 19 Co-Authors
From Around the World

www.jdnpublications.com

ISBN: 978-1-938432-56-9 (Paperback)

ISBN: 978-1-938432-57-6 (Ebook)

Copyright © 2025 Among Friends, Inspiring And Impactful Stories From the Soul

Written by Edna L Isaac alongside 19 co-authors from around the world:

Alfaxad Sánchez, Claudia P. Álvarez, Dinora Puello, Dorothy Álvarez, Elizabeth Puello, Elizabeth Walcott, Erica V. Figueroa, Ester Delvillar, Gerianne Marra, Jeannett Toro, Jenny Fortes, Judith De la Espriella, Judian Bartolomey, Keren Sánchez, María Ligia Callejas, Marisol Martínez, Marisol Severino, Nilsa M. Ortiz, Sheila Dávila.

All rights reserved.

No part of this book may be reproduced in any form without the written permission of the publisher or author, except as permitted by United States copyright law.

Disclaimer

JDN/EDUCATE Publishing is a self-publishing platform that offers authors the opportunity to publish their works without going through an editorial selection process. The authors are responsible for the content of their works, and in particular, JDN/EDUCATE does not necessarily agree with the content of this book. We are not responsible for errors in it, and we do not assume any responsibility for the consequences of reading it. Readers should be aware that the content of this book is the sole responsibility of the author.

Front and Back Cover designed by JDN PUBLICATIONS. Background photo for front and back cover created by AI from canva.com.

Printed in the United States of America

A Note To The Reader

　　We direct these words to you, who hold this book in your hands at this very moment. To each of our readers, regardless of age, gender, or social status. If you have opened these pages, it is because the Heavenly Father has guided you to them with the promise that here you will find the echo of His truth, a reflection of His love, and the empathy He has sown into each of these stories. A Supportive Embrace from the Father.

　　To you, friend, who life has struck hard. To you who, in the silence of the night, soak your pillow with tears before finding rest. To you who fully trusted and gave yourself, only to receive a betrayal that left a deep wound, one from which it has been so difficult to heal. We want you to know that you are not alone. In every narrative of this book, you will find the reflection of twenty courageous and honest voices that, by weaving together their sorrows and joys, remind you that life's challenges are not faced in isolation, but with the company of God. This book is a warm and supportive embrace from the Holy Spirit for each one of you, a community of souls beating at the same rhythm. It is a beacon of hope lit from our collective soul, designed to heal and inspire with the light of Christ. A Journey of Healing with Divine Purpose.

　　May the empathy, understanding, and fellowship that await you in these pages inspire you to move forward, to heal, and to flourish. May you succeed, hand-in-hand with God, in transforming every pain into strength and every step into proof of resilience and overcoming. May you not only discover stories here but also the strength He has given you to forge your own path. May you find the certainty that, in Him, and together in His Kingdom, we are stronger. May this book be the reminder that our echo, when shared, resonates beyond the individual soul, leaving an indelible mark on the world for the glory of God.

Among Friends

DEDICATED

First to the Father, Son, and Holy Spirit, then to a great Friend

To A Friend

To one of my mentors, friend, counselor, fellow warrior, and so much more. To you, Pastor Ramonita Díaz, with much love and respect, for your humility, dedication, and everything you contribute to the Kingdom of God and to the expansion of the gospel.

~Edna

∽

At all times, a friend loves,
And he is like a brother in times of distress.
(Literary translation from the Spanish KJV Version)

Proverbs 17:17

∽

*Thank you very much! To you,
Pastor Ramonita Díaz, With much love and respect.*

Born in Puerto Rico, but having resided in Boston, Massachusetts, for the greater part of her life, this woman has been a profound example in my life and deserves all my respect, as does her family. She has worked diligently, not only as a **spiritual authority** *in Boston and its surrounding areas, but she has also dedicated many years of her life to the community, working for the Boston Public Schools Department. Furthermore, she is a member of the Executive Board of the Pastors' Fellowship in New England and has served on the board of directors for various organizations in the area.*

Her labor in the work of the Lord has been exemplary and impressive. Her radio program on Radio Luz touched and impacted thousands of lives for **seven consecutive years**. *She is widely known for her program Para Esta Hora (For This Hour), which transformed countless hearts. Nevertheless, her* **humility** *and her genuine approach to people have always distinguished her.*

I remember that upon meeting her, I immediately felt as if we had known each other all our lives. She is the only person who can tell me every truth, scold me fiercely, and insult me if she wishes, and I would not be offended; on the contrary, every word that comes from her mouth is used by God for my benefit. The praise for the virtuous woman of Proverbs 31:10-31 is fulfilled in her, especially the verse that says:

> **She openeth her mouth with wisdom;**
> **And the law of kindness is on her tongue. (Proverbs 31;26)**

When I met her and asked many leaders if anyone had honored her, I was surprised to learn that they had not yet done so. Therefore, I decided to honor her with a **special recognition** *in the JDN magazine, surprising her with her photo on the cover and pages dedicated to her biography. She nearly "killed me," as she did not know that the questions*

I was asking her during a conversation were, in fact, an interview for the magazine.

*I did it with great respect and love, knowing that if I had mentioned it, she would not have allowed it. Pastor Ramonita prefers to maintain her anonymity (for example, she declined when I invited her to be a co-author of this book). But I deeply believe in the **law of honor**, and a servant so wise who has done so much for the Lord's work deserves our respect and honor **during her lifetime**, and not just after her passing.*

*Since she first heard the mission and vision of JDN PUBLICATIONS, she has always honored us, being one of our **greatest collaborators**. Her distinction cannot be overlooked. Although I know she does not like to be mentioned, she has always believed in JDN, advised us, and has **invested time, wisdom, and love** in our ministry.*

Thank you very much, Pastor Ramonita, for being who you are and for always giving your best. I pray that God will raise up thousands or millions of "Ramonitas" globally who are willing to share the Word and the passion for the Pauline letters as you do.

*For all this, and much more, we dedicate this book to you with much love, as well as our **Entre Amigas 2025** conference, under the theme: **"Woman, God Has Already Written Your Story."***

Marisol Martinez
Boston, MA

PROLOGUE

Beyond the "I"

Redefining Friendship

Among Friends

BEYOND THE "I":
REDEFINING FRIENDSHIP
BY MARISOL MARTÍNEZ, BOSTON, MA

The first thing that comes to mind when I hear the word *"friend"* is an admiration for those who enjoy the benefit of a genuine friendship. These individuals have been mutually rewarded by giving and receiving life through a sincere and reciprocal friendship. When I say they have "given and received life," I mean it in the context expressed by Christ in John 15:13: "Greater love has no one than this, than to lay down one's life for his friends."

But did Jesus mean this literally? While it is possible for someone to literally sacrifice their life for another, I do `not believe Christ was exclusively referring to literal death. Because the Bible is not a matter of private interpretation and interprets itself, Paul's statement in Galatians 2:20 explains that it is not about dying physically, but about dying to our old way of life so that Christ may live in us.

In the case of laying down our lives for our friends, it refers to the death of our selfishness, our self-interest. Scholars claim that the Greek word for friend, philos, is related to the concepts of "without" (philia is often used for love, but the philosophical etymology plays on a- "without" and ego "self," though linguistically debatable, the spiritual meaning holds true here), suggesting a meaning of "without my self." I therefore understand that a true friend, when faced with the demands of this role, sets aside her agenda, her desires, her opinion, her ego—the list could be infinitely long—for the sole purpose of making herself present.

There are moments when talking is unnecessary, and simply being present speaks louder than a thousand words. A friend listens to affirm that we are not alone, which is very different from one who listens hastily, ready to offer a response before we have finished speaking.

Returning to John 15:13, it is easier and more convenient to send an expensive gift than make a visit. Giving our time seems to be an impossible act, a sacrifice reserved for matters of life or death. The problem is our inability to recognize that giving 15 minutes of ourselves may be the equivalent of saving another life. I believe that what Jesus meant by "to lay down one's life for his friends" is equivalent to being "without myself."

The language of our innovative times and social media has degraded the meaning of the word "friend." Everyone is "friends" with everyone on social media, but this superficial connection does not deserve the term, which encapsulates such a profound meaning and demands expectations far beyond the perfect picture we post online.

I hold a strong conviction about what a friend should be, which is why I cannot use the word lightly or to refer to most women I have met. A friend should not suffer alone. If you have the privilege of a friend, there is no reason for you to cross the desert without someone you can call to pour out your heart when the scorching sun suffocates you, or when the cold, dark night fills you with fear and hopelessness.

I admire those women who have sustained a friendship for years and together have reached a season where memories continue to strengthen their bonds. Many of us have not been so fortunate—some because we did not know how to cultivate that friendship, others because our upbringing left us incapable of building such friendly ties, and still others because rejection is inevitable when certain fundamental principles are not shared. I am not referring to differences of opinion; I speak of a lifestyle rejected by people who consequently reject those who adopt it.

During a women's meeting, we were discussing what it means to be a woman of God. Among the comments, one that powerfully stood out was that a woman of God does not have many friends. This may seem contradictory and difficult to process at first, but when you analyze the depth of that statement, you will conclude that the uncommon nature of a woman of God's character is neither common nor popular among others.

The characteristics of a woman of God—which are not limited to loyalty, confidentiality, empathy, tolerance, and the courage to say what a person needs to hear, not just what they want to hear—are ingredients that do not produce many friends.

Regrettably, a reality of being a woman of God is often walking alone; however, a different perspective would turn us into an invincible army against the fight with loneliness, discouragement, sickness, or personal problems that make us vulnerable and confirm that "it is not good for man to be alone" (Genesis 2:18). We were created to live in community. Even the strongest and most independent person needs other human beings. After God had created everything, he noticed something that was not right. Adam enjoyed all creation and was accompanied by all the animals he himself had named; nevertheless, God said, "It is not good that the man should be alone" (Genesis 2:18). This declaration does not refer exclusively to a marital context, as we regularly interpret it, but to the context that we need one another. We were created to dwell in the company of other human beings. A pet can alleviate loneliness and provide emotional support, but all the animals in the then-created world were not enough to satisfy Adam's need for community.

How I would like to share a personal experience that highlights the loyalty and companionship of someone in my life whom I could genuinely and proudly call a "friend." Someone whose presence throughout the years has proven the fidelity and reciprocal, unconditional love that defines true friendship. Unfortunately, this is not the case. This does not mean that I haven't had, or do not have, people in my life I can count on for a favor or an immediate need. On the contrary, I am grateful for many people who are helpful and willing, but are they "friends"?

That word is reserved for those women who suddenly appear unannounced because they know you are going through a period in your journey when you need to know you have a friend; for the woman who celebrates your achievements, who reaffirms your potential when you fall short of a goal, and for the one who unreservedly confronts you when you need correction.

Among friends, we cry, we laugh, and we recognize that we must stop being "self," if only for a moment, so that another may receive life. It is not about sending a text message two or three times a year that reads "Merry Christmas," "Happy Mother's Day," etc.—that is nothing more than a superficial, cybernetic acquaintance, far from the reality of true friendship.

Time passes faster than we realize, especially when we are younger and have a greater opportunity to establish bonds of friendship. Suddenly, we realize that we did not invest enough in certain areas of our lives. If I could go back, I would make sure to value and cultivate friendships that would walk with me throughout this journey we call life. We were created to live in fellowship with one another, and what better fellowship than that which can exist between friends.

Let's Learn More About Marisol Martinez

MARISOL IS the author of the book "Cuando La Vida Sucede" (When Life Happens). Although I have not known her for many years, the brief time we have conversed has been enough to give me testimony of a great woman of God. Her words impacted me deeply because they contain a great truth, especially for those of us who do not have many friends or when ministry becomes a lonely path, as not everyone comprehends our vision and purpose in the Lord. In fact, I had to use her words in the Preface of this book, as they capture the profound essence of "Entre Amigas" (Among Friends). These are words that resonate deep in the heart and help us redefine true Friendship. Thank you, Marisol, for your powerful words.

Marisol Martínez was born in the Dominican Republic and lived in New York when her family emigrated to the United States at the age of 12. As a businesswoman, she possesses diverse skills and experiences that include, among others, pastoral ministry, church planting, parent-school liaison, real estate agent, interpreter, wife, and homemaker. However, her greatest triumph was raising three children who are now a great resource to today's society. Having been widowed after more than 30 years of marriage, Marisol now enjoys the joy and blessing imparted by her grandchildren and the satisfaction of three accomplished children.

By Edna L Isaac
Taunton, MA

Introduction

Friendship or Betrayal? If Only I Had Listened

FRIENDSHIP OR BETRAYAL? HAD I ONLY LISTENED

BY EDNA L. ISAAC, TAUNTON, MA

This book you hold in your hands isn't just a collection of pages; it's a collective embrace, a living testament to the transcendent power of what God can do in the lives of many of us. But what is true friendship really? As the biblical wisdom in Proverbs 17:17 reminds us:

"A friend loves at all times, and a brother is born for adversity."

In this space, diverse female voices from around the world converge to offer you a refuge, a mirror, and a renewed sense of purpose. These are stories born of the soul, forged in experience, and distilled into knowledge, ready to resonate with you and impact your life profoundly. I've always maintained that, as we journey through life, we encounter different situations that often cause trauma.

We often long for wise counsel, a hand to uplift us, a voice that understands us, relief from pain, and unconditional support—in short, a true friendship, which is difficult to find.

We crave those words that unveil the hidden pain behind tragedy, betrayal, deception, or illness. Words like those God offered me for a young woman facing adversity, which today form the soul of Entre Amigas Internacional (Among Friends International):

Sister Friend Be my eyes, when I cannot see the danger. Be my hands, when I cannot reach the need, Be my feet, when I cannot walk to the set goal. Be my voice when my feelings I cannot express. Be my shoulder to cry on when I face the pain. Be the back that carries me when I can no longer go on. Friend, I need you, and I will do the same for you.

Inspired by the Holy Spirit, and written by Edna L. Isaac

Prepare to be inspired, moved, and strengthened by these narratives that celebrate the connection, resilience, and profound sisterhood of Entre Amigas, a movement that God is raising around the world for this last season. Open these pages and discover the transformative power of stories shared from the deepest part of the soul.

In fact, I want to share just a little about how God gave me these "Sister Friend" words. With the permission of the person I will be discussing, I share with you an experience that you must not only hear with your ears but also listen to with your heart. For none of us—including the men reading this book—are exempt from having something like this happen to us; therefore, let us pray for those who have lived through it.

The Echo of a Broken Heart

IT WAS **two in the morning** when the sudden vibration of my phone jolted me out of a deep sleep. A pang of unrest shot through my soul; I knew, in the deepest part of my heart, that only a **desperate emergency** would dare to break the silence of the night. With trembling hands, I picked up the phone, and the screen lit up with a message that chilled me to the bone.

An **emoji of inconsolable weeping** accompanied the words that were etched into my soul:

> 😭😭😭 "Forgive me, Pastor, for not following your advice.
>
> So-and-so had me arrested, accused me of Attempted Murder, took my children away, and is now with her. They described her to me; they see her entering my house every day—it's her!" 😭

IT WAS the shattered voice of a broken heart. The voice of a 24-year-old young mother whom I had warned over and over about the shadow looming over her life. She had fallen into the abyss of manipulation, deceit, and physical, emotional, and psychological abuse.

But the most gut-wrenching part, the most vile betrayal: that of her husband with her "best friend," the godmother of her own children, and, to top it off, a "sister" in the faith who attended the same congregation.

Although this young couple had sincerely and passionately served God since their reconciliation with Him, a spiritual crack in their home allowed the enemy to infiltrate. Despite my constant warnings—divine revelations about hidden sin and tireless prayers—they paid no heed.

Unwillingly, she allowed herself to be dragged into Satan's traps, manipulated by the one who should have loved her and by the one who called herself her friend, plunging into a whirlpool of lies, deception, and betrayal.

I remember confronting them with wisdom and a mother's heart, advising them to separate themselves from this couple who would only bring them affliction. However, my warnings fell on deaf ears. Sadly, our advice and pleas were ignored.

We cannot force anyone; we are merely instruments in God's hands, but each person is responsible for their own decisions. Sometimes, love blinds us, foolishness drags us down, ignorance deceives us, or fear paralyzes us, preventing us from seeing the precipice others are anxiously pointing out. How much I regret that she didn't listen to me!

Our mission as servants is to offer the light of counsel, not to impose it. If someone offers you a guiding hand born of divine wisdom, please, listen closely. They could be the eyes you need when your own vision is obscured by pain or confusion.

This young mother was the victim of a Machiavellian conspiracy. Her husband and her supposed best friend plotted to destroy her and steal her children, leveraging their own knowledge of family law, divorce, and legal custody. Despite the atrocious pain they inflicted, they persisted in their deceit, even feigning devotion in church while their hearts harbored the premeditated destruction of an innocent life.

Although we do not judge the past, the bitter fruit reveals the true nature. Those who persist in lying and causing harm, even hiding behind faith, distance themselves from grace until there is genuine repentance and sincere reparation. I firmly believe in divine forgiveness, but also in the imperative need to mend the wrong caused, especially when the offense is still active.

Hence, the vital importance of alerts in our relationships, particularly those based on trust. Wise counsel must be heard; advice offered with truth and acceptance of reality must be heeded. Let us not ignore the divine warnings that come to us through others.

This is how the words of our international ministry were born. One morning, before accompanying this young woman to court as she fought for her innocence against false charges, I begged God:

"Please, let me feel the burden of this girl, everything she is going through."

I never imagined that God would literally allow me to feel a weight so overwhelming that it doubled me over. I was astonished at how she, despite everything, was still standing. I truly couldn't believe she still maintained her sanity and sound judgment. I could feel her suffering, step into her shoes for an instant, and I wouldn't wish on my worst enemy what this young woman was enduring.

For this reason, it was essential to begin with this painful story, because from it emerged the heart of Entre Amigas. Let us help others to see what they cannot see, to carry them on our shoulders when they can barely walk, to intercede for them with groans too deep for words when they have no tears left, only silent weeping.

Let us not judge them when we see that anguish and betrayal push them to desperation. Let us use empathy, because, as the old saying goes, "No one knows what is in the pot but the spoon that stirs it." Let us not judge the reaction to betrayal; empathy reminds us that only the one living the experience knows its depth.

Thus, the words God gave me that morning for that young woman, which are now the motto of our Entre Amigas International Ministry, invite us to action: to be their feet when they cannot walk toward the set goal.

To be their mouth when pain and suffering silence their feelings. Let us be their shoulder to cry on during affliction, without judging them, without condemning them, and certainly without murmuring, "I told you so."

In that moment, what they need is for us to be the back that carries them when the burden is unbearable and they can no longer continue. Today, they need us, but as the old saying goes, "Today for them, tomorrow for us."

We want to share with you a new collection of writings; stories from the soul that will resonate with you, inspiring and deeply moving you. We begin this journey alongside our first co-author and her beautiful story. We hope that these narratives of faith, resilience, and lived experiences will be a source of edification and comfort for you.

If you are passionate about helping other women, writing, lecturing, preaching, teaching, or have something to give, don't hold back, and we are here to help you achieve your dreams—contact us and be part of our JDN Global Leadership Network team, our team of editors and writers, collaborators, and much more: find us on social media or on our websites:

JDN PUBLICATIONS https://jdnpublications.com/ https://www.jdncorporation.com/ Email: jdncpublications@gmail.com Office: 508-681-3115 Cell: 774-444-7268 If you wish to host our Entre Amigas Internacional conferences, please contact us by writing to: entreamigasint@gmail.com. Find us on our platforms and get in touch with us.

Let's Learn More About Edna L. Isaac

EDNA ISAAC WAS BORN in Aguadilla, Puerto Rico, and moved to the United States at age 16, settling in Massachusetts. She has been married to Francisco J. Isaac for 34 years, and they have four children. Edna is a multifaceted figure, known as a professional change agent, author, and international speaker.

She is the CEO and President of JDN Corporation and JDN Publications / EDUCATE Publishing, based in Taunton, MA, with an impact that extends internationally. She is the co-founder and associate pastor of the Iglesia Casa de Adoración or CDA House of Worship in Taunton, MA, which she leads alongside her husband. She is also the founder of: Radio WHUC 95.6 FM (currently under construction); Entre Amigas Internacional, a ministry dedicated to healing, empowering, and preaching; Association of Christian Churches and Ministries Inc; and JDN Global Leadership Network. Furthermore, Edna is an active figure in her community and in academic circles. She previously presided over the Taunton, MA, and surrounding areas Clergy Association for seven years and was also a professor for five years, teaching theology at

ETME, a ministerial school in Boston, MA, and 6 years at the Assemblies of God Institute in New Bedford.

She currently works as a Senior Counselor at one of the Community Justice Support Centers in MA. As an author, she has written over 13 books. Her most recent book is "Refinados Como El Oro" (Refined As Gold). For more information, you can visit www.jdnpublications.com and www.jdncorporation.com or contact her via email at: jdncpublications@gmail.com.

Judith De la Espriella
Republic of Panamá

FIRST
STORY

TO MY BELOVED AND BEAUTIFUL HOLY SPIRIT MY FAITHFUL COMPANION

Among Friends

1

TO MY BELOVED AND BEAUTIFUL HOLY SPIRIT, MY FAITHFUL COMPANION

PASTOR JUDITH DE LA ESPRIELLA DE GIL, REPUBLIC OF PANAMÁ

I want to testify to the love and faithfulness of my Beloved Holy Spirit—that beautiful Person who arrived in my life on Friday, December 24, 2004, 20 years ago. At that time, I felt lost, without a reason to live, surrounded by all material comforts but burdened with an empty life, a great sadness and solitude, with no desire to continue, wondering what my purpose was, why I existed, and why I lived on this earth.

During those days, I was given the book Traveling Light by Max Lucado, which the Holy Spirit began to use as a tool to speak to me. As I read, I felt the process of healing in my heart, reaching deep inside me like a loving and gentle scalpel. It flooded the most secret parts of my life, healing my wounds and painful memories, and ministering the grace to forgive myself and all those who had been a part of and surrounded my life since I was a young child.

I finished reading the book in just a couple of days, and I immediately fell to my knees, asking my Heavenly Father for forgiveness for my sins and accepting Jesus as the Lord and Savior of my life. From that moment, my new life began, along with my Christian walk under the total and complete direction of my beloved and beautiful Holy Spirit, my Divine Paraclete who walks with me—my Helper, my Counselor, my Comforter, my Exhorter, my Faithful Friend.

My experiences and testimonies of my relationship with the Holy Spirit are unique. My delight in the Holy Spirit is unique. Through worship and music, there is an immense and intense surrender and desire for His presence, in accordance with Psalm 37:4:

> "Delight yourself in the LORD, and he will give you the desires of your heart."

I decrease so that He may increase and use me through the ministry of worship, so that He may minister to people's hearts; so that He may heal the brokenhearted; so that He may set captives free; restore sight to the blind, and release the oppressed.

In accordance with the Word of God, Psalm 100 says:

> *1 Shout for joy to the LORD, all the earth. 2 Worship the LORD with gladness; come before him with joyful songs. 3 Know that the LORD is God. It is he who made us, and we are his. We are his people, sheep in his meadows. 4 Enter his gates with thanksgiving and his courts with praise. Give thanks and praise his name. 5 For the LORD is good and his love endures forever; his faithfulness continues through all generations.*

The Holy Spirit has made everything new in me. He burst into my life at age 50. Throughout these 20 years of having welcomed Him into my life and serving Him, under His guidance and direction, I have been happily married for 18 years to my beloved husband, Pastor Priciano Gil Hernández. Together, we pastor the

Ministerio Internacional Jesús es Vida (Jesus is Life International Ministry) in Panama City, Republic of Panama.

I want to tell you, who are reading me, whatever the situation you may be facing, I want to introduce you to my Beloved and Beautiful Holy Spirit,

He is your Comforter and Helper, SEEK HIM AND KNOW HIM. HE WILL HELP YOU AND WILL BE WITH YOU FOREVER.

The Holy Spirit is a Person about whom Jesus said it was better for Him to go away, because if He did not go, the Comforter would not come to us, but if He went, He would send Him to be with us forever.

"But the Comforter, the Holy Spirit, whom the Father will send in my name, he will teach you all things, and bring to your remembrance all that I have said to you."

"When the Spirit of truth comes, he will guide you into all the truth." The Holy Spirit reveals Jesus Christ to us and is the one who will lead us day by day to the stature of the perfect man, JESUS CHRIST, the author and finisher of our faith.

Pastor Judith De la Espriella de Gil
Servant of the Lord

PASTOR JUDITH HAS BEEN SERVING for twenty years and has been happily married for eighteen years to her beloved husband, Pastor Priciano Gil Hernández. Together, they pastor the Ministerio Internacional Jesús es Vida in Panama City, Republic of Panama, dedicated to guiding others to know the Lord. I met this humble yet great woman of God the first time we held the Entre Amigas Internacional Women Conference. They opened the doors of their congregation to us, and while I was there preparing for the first day of conferences, God spoke to me and said, "Do you know why I allowed you to hold Entre Amigas here in Panama first? Because it is a prophetic event, Panama is a bridge between continents, and Entre Amigas will reach all continents." Wow, that event marked my life. The humility of Pastor Judith and her beloved husband, Pastor Gil—now the president of the Evangelical Alliance of Panama—is evident. Pastor Judith also leads the women's ministry nationally and internationally. Together with her beloved husband, they travel throughout Panama and other parts of the world, bringing the Word through conferences, events, marches, and meetings that unite Pastors, congregations, and leaders to make a difference and fight for the rights that represent the sound and transformative Gospel. Their ministry has touched not only the Christian community but also the spheres of the Panamanian government. I love them in the Lord and wish them much success.

SECOND
STORY

STEADFAST BETWEEN CHAOS AND PURPOSE

Gerriane Marra
Taunton, MA

2

STEADFAST AMIDST THE CHAOS AND THE PURPOSE

BY GERRIANE MARRA, RAYNHAM, MA

Forgiving to Achieve Peace

How many times have we asked, "Why me, God?" and expected an answer promising to make everything better, only to hear God say, "Why not you?" It may not be the answer we want, but it is often the one we need.

WHEN you ask yourself WHY, know this: You stand firm BETWEEN the CHAOS and the PURPOSE!

In my own life, I have faced great trials, to say the least. Forty-seven years of domestic abuse that began at age three, being stabbed by my mother, two suicide attempts, assault, beatings, and rape in my own home, along with other hardships.

I have also been deeply affected by the knowledge of the persecution and torture of those in Pakistan who believe in Jesus Christ, including people I have met and consider friends. The horrific realities of abuse, beatings, nails piercing bodies, being burned alive... the appalling situations we encounter in life, from those we know, with whom we associate, even those we have never personally met—How do we deal with all of that?

High levels of defilement, abuse, abandonment, anger, hatred, bitterness, rage, disobedience, and vengeance had taken over my mind, body, and heart. I simply couldn't continue living that way. From my parents and siblings to acquaintances, distant people, and even strangers who have experienced similar feelings and problems... what is left for healing?

It's called GRACE

The bottom line is that we must SURRENDER and FORGIVE! Forgiveness is a difficult pill to swallow, at least it was for me. My human nature instinctively wanted to retaliate, to get even, to inflict some form of harmful retribution—a role that is not ours to play. People can be awful, selfish, and cruel, but we are still called to give them a chance... It's called GRACE.

The same GRACE that God has given and continues to give us. We are not God, but we are commanded to act accordingly in this difficult world. Give people a chance... sometimes they may surprise you.

We must also understand that UNFORGIVENESS holds us hostage. It imprisons our thoughts, our actions, and even our health. Without our knowing it, it invades us like a silent disease, spreading from the inside out.

We walk with bitterness, jealousy, abandonment, anger, hatred, and a tangle of other negative emotions. Even when we believe we have untangled ourselves from our situations and resolved the issues, the animosity we harbor only makes things worse, allowing the infection to fester and spread within.

I know that UNFORGIVENESS is a persistent spiritual force that constantly torments us, drawing us further away from our relationship with God. The enemy seeks to steal our inheritance.

A truth I hold onto is that FORGIVENESS is for me, not for

the one who offended me. Forgive others, not because they deserve it, but because you deserve peace.

What I realized is that FORGIVENESS is a CHOICE; it is a DECISION OF MY WILL! IT IS NOT AN EMOTION! It's not that I cannot forgive; it is that I do not want to.

How many tears I shed for my disobedience. God never asked me to forgive Him, since I was the one who offended Him. What audacity!

All you feel is the offense you committed against God. God is WHOM you disobeyed!

Even in the many times I asked God to take away this pain, to guide me in how He wanted to deliver me from this DISEASE that was attacking my body, my focus should have been on "Him, not me."

I left the door open to spiritual, emotional, mental, and even physical attacks through my own wrong actions, choices, and will —not His.

GOD will NEVER oppose man's will. Unforgiveness can take a severe toll on your physical body. I am living proof of that. God's love is sacrificial. As it says in 1 John 4:10:

"In this is love, not that we loved God, but that He loved us and sent His Son to be the propitiation for our sins." And Romans 8:1 declares: "There is therefore now no condemnation to those who are in Christ Jesus, who do not walk according to the flesh, but according to the Spirit."

NO condemnation—that is, NEVER! No guilty verdict, no punishment for us to bear. WHY?

Because WE have offended God, then who are WE to not forgive others? What we have done against God might be unforgivable.

Guilt, shame, bitterness, anger, and other toxic emotions are not spirits with whom we should be in contact or communication. We must serve God.

It is our disobedience and unwillingness to move forward that keeps us captive, preventing God from hearing us or our prayers.

As long as you serve those negative spirits, you will remain bound. We cannot serve two masters. Only through obedience, faith in God's Word, not clinging to past wounds, and trusting God can those chains be broken.

We often go against everything God tells us in His Word about who we are. With whom have you been conversing? What voice or voices are you listening to? Whose report do you believe? You have the CHOICE. You have the DECISION. It is your WILL... FORGIVE! WALK TOWARD YOUR PEACE! BE RENEWED! LET GO AND GROW! DELIVERANCE TO PEACE!

Let us pray this prayer aloud

Dear God,

I accept your forgiveness and no longer hold onto the wrongdoings of the past. Thank You, Jesus, for bringing godly men and women into my life, who have been stepping stones amidst the stumbles I have experienced, to help me, counsel me, pray for me, and guide me through these burdens. Thank You, Jesus, for forgiving me now for choosing my will. I choose to forgive everyone who has hurt me in so many ways. I forgive them and surrender them to You. Master, I command every evil spirit that has taken advantage of me to leave me now in Jesus' Name. I release myself, by the choice of my will, from being a victim held in the bondage of these wrong actions any longer. I declare my freedom from all resentment, anger, bitterness, shame, guilt, abandonment, jealousy, depression, and anything else You have shown me on my healing journey. Heal my memories and my broken heart from the evil done to me, and let every broken part of my soul leave now as I surrender everything to You, Lord, for restoration. I release all of this as I thank You that Your healing virtues flow throughout my body, mind, and spirit as I receive Your love. In Your Precious Name, I pray. Because YOU OWE ME NOTHING, BUT I OWE YOU EVERYTHING, AND I THANK YOU. AMEN.

Let's Learn More About Gerriane Marra

GERRIANE IS A WOMAN OF FAITH, passionate about everything she undertakes in the work of the Lord. Despite her physical limitations, I have witnessed her incredible dedication. Among the many services she has offered in her community for many years, she was the mastermind and driving force behind the success of a local food pantry, serving the community with dedication.

Furthermore, Gerriane volunteered for many years in programs like the YMCA and taught children after school hours, generously sharing her talent and knowledge. She also devoted her time to her local church, giving without expecting anything in return.

Thank you, Gerriane, for your beautiful words and for sharing part of your testimony.

Among Friends

THIRD
STORY

GOD TRANSFORMS HEARTHS

DINORA PUELLO
DOMINICAN REPUBLIC

3

GOD TRANSFORMS HEARTS
BY DINORA PUELLO, SANTO DOMINGO

May the grace and peace of God abundantly bless every person who reads these lines. May this testimony be for the edification of your lives. On Sunday, April 20, 2025, on this day, the Lord inspires me to write to exalt and bless the name of Jesus. Psalm 103:10 reminds us of His immense mercy:

> "He does not deal with us according to our sins, nor repay us according to our iniquities."

I am in awe of the way God extended His great mercy toward a cousin whose character was exceedingly difficult and aggressive. She was an impenetrable and untamable person, and although she had been raised in a Christian home with her mother and aunt, she seemed to have experienced a trauma that turned her into an enemy of the world, especially of her mother, her aunt, and even me. She wanted nothing to do with me and waged a strong war against her mother and aunt.

Following their passing, my cousin was left alone with her son.

Then, he too left, plunging her into deep depression and making her even more rebellious.

It was then that God began to deal with me through videos of His servants Yiye Ávila and Juan Carlos Harrigan, teaching me how to pray and intercede for our relatives who are far from the Lord.

In the year 2020, I began to cry out to God with tears and groans for my cousin, persevering in fasting and supplication. God spoke to me more and more in dreams, showing me that the enemy wanted to destroy her. This intensified my crying out and my petition to the Lord for her deliverance. In my visions, I saw how demons were trying to take her away.

The Lord began to reveal my cousin's needs to me. She had become very poor and lonely. Then, the love of God began to flow in my heart toward her, even though I didn't know how to approach her life.

God opened a door for me in 2020 with the birth of her granddaughter. She started to smile, and I took that opportunity to invite her to a nearby church that had just opened its doors. I shared with her what God had shown me, but she remained imposing and proud, her mind still in chains. Her house reflected her internal state, filled with garbage, bottles, and newspapers; she was a compulsive buyer.

I began to prophesy to her that God would liberate and bless her. On two occasions, at 2:00 a.m., I heard the voice of God urgently calling me to intercede for her. I saw how they were trying to destroy her.

In 2021, I made an urgent petition to the Lord from the depths of my heart: that my cousin would convert to Christ and that her only son would meet his father, who had only visited him when he was a baby.

God answered my prayer, and three months later, on May 25, 2021, her son's father appeared, and she accepted Christ with tears.

A young teenage girl who was preaching made the altar call, and my cousin surrendered to Christ, weeping. My faith grew tremendously.

Shortly after, her son discovered that his mother was ill and informed me. I was able to take her to the doctor, where she was diagnosed with breast cancer. We began to care for her; my sister Esther took her to her medical appointments, and God opened financial doors to provide for her needs.

Her transformation was extraordinary. She began to smile more and more and preached the Gospel to those who visited her.

She was no longer the aggressive woman who cursed and fought. She asked forgiveness from people she had offended. One of her worst enemies testified in the neighborhood that "Belice had changed" and said, "God changes people!"

Her house was cleaned and restored, just like her life. During a very difficult health trial, she was able to tell me, "Dinorah, don't worry, you and I are going to come out victorious from this!"

One day she told me that she felt the Lord's gentle hand pass over her head and arms. She began to advise us not to worry about anything, and her face became like that of a child.

On one occasion, the enemy tried to provoke her anger, but the Lord immediately sent help and restored her peace. I asked her if she wasn't afraid to sleep alone, and she replied, "I am not afraid. The Lord took away my fear, anxiety, and rage. I sleep peacefully."

Neighbors and relatives were astonished by what was happening. Despite the breast cancer, she gave thanks to God every day. She began to pray for all the people who offered her help and to give thanks, saying, "Thank you, Lord, for showing me Your love. I didn't know God loved me so much. Thank you for placing people to help me."

She asked for forgiveness daily from the people around her, including her son. The most surprising thing is that they lacked nothing; everything was abundant. She did not suffer any need.

She told everyone, "Repent, Christ is coming!" She even sent for a sorcerer to preach the Gospel to her.

She taught us not to complain about our situations so that things would not become more complicated.

Then, God began to prepare my mind. He sent pastors to anoint her with oil. Her mind became as innocent as that of a child; it was a new birth, a new person.

It was very painful for me and my sister Esther, but we had the privilege of seeing her depart with the Lord without complaint, in peace, because she experienced a new birth. Because God changes hearts!

Her pastors baptized her in 2023. I thank God for the generous hands and for those who came to pray with her.

Let's Learn More About Dinora Puello

DINORA IS a servant of God who has known and served God most of her life. With her impeccable testimony and great love, she preaches on the streets with a speaker and intercedes in prayer for others. I met her on my first trip to Santo Domingo, and her humility and devotion to God impacted my life in such a way that she will always have a very special place in my heart. She does not seek the spotlight, and perhaps she has been ignored or despised by many, but her voice and intercession are well-known in Heaven. When we were in Santo Domingo, we had the privilege of going out with her to evangelize and pray for people on the streets.

Thank you, beloved Dinora, for the beautiful testimony you have shared with us. May God continue to use your life to touch multitudes; although your name may not resonate on social media, it does resonate at the Throne. Go forward in the Lord!

FOURTH
STORY

THIS CLAUDIA SHE DOESN'T GIVE UP

Claudia P. Álvarez
Lakeville, MA

4

THIS CLAUDIA DOES NOT GIVE UP

BY CLAUDIA PATRICIA ÁLVAREZ, LAKEVILLE, MA

One day, I promised myself I would not give up. Since then, I repeat to myself with strength and tenderness: This Claudia does not give up. And it is not just a phrase; it is an act of spiritual resistance, of vital drive, and of blind faith in a God who has never let go of my hand, even when my human strength was exhausted.

My story has a before and an after marked by pain and transformation. In 1994, an accident to my spine changed the course of my life. I moved a very heavy bed, and that simple, everyday act unleashed a chain of surgeries: five operations that brought me face-to-face with my physical and emotional limits. I had dreams like anyone: I longed to build a beautiful home, full of love, and when I first married, I felt it was more than I had imagined.

Doctors warned me that a pregnancy would be a very high risk. But God, in His perfect sovereignty, gifted me with my daughter Verónica. She arrived as light, as a promise, as a driving force.

However, one day, that castle crumbled in the most absurd way, and with it, my emotional and spiritual stability. The loss was devastating, and I was forced to rebuild myself from the rubble. So, I decided to take flight and cross borders.

I arrived in this country not knowing that I would have to say goodbye to my parents. It was one of the greatest pains I have ever lived through. When my mother became ill, another spinal surgery awaited me. She herself begged me not to travel without having the operation first. She told me in a soft but firm voice:

> "Don't worry, daughter. God is going to give me the strength to wait for you. After you have the surgery, you come, and you will see that I myself will go to meet you at the airport."

However, that day never came. The surgery became complicated, and the doctor himself forbade me from traveling. Exactly one month later, my mother passed away in the presence of the Lord. Not being able to say goodbye to her was an indescribable blow. But even in that pain, God sustained me. He taught me that His presence transcends distance, that there are eternal hugs given through prayer, and that love is not broken even by death.

Being in another country, without speaking English, seemed like another wall. How could I move forward if I couldn't even communicate? But when God opens doors, no language can close His purpose. I started working in my local school district. I remember that when I told my family I was going to work where no one spoke Spanish, they burst out laughing:

"Claudia Patricia, you are crazy! How are you going to work there without speaking English?" And I replied with a smile: "Well, it was God who led me there, so it is His problem to solve it."

Today, ten years later, I am still in the same place. I have found favor with my colleagues and, most beautifully, I work with the special education department. This experience has transformed me. It has made me more human, more empathetic, more sensitive. And much more full of faith.

Along the way, love came again. I married a wonderful man, for whom, 20 years later, I am still his queen. My son, Alejandro, was born, and with his sister, Verónica, they became the center of my life. My husband and I call ourselves the Iron Team. Together we have faced two strokes he suffered, and today, more than ever, I can say: I feel strong, renewed, determined. God has been faithful.

I had the material for my books stored for years, waiting for the right moment. One day I understood that this was the way God wanted to use me, and my books were born: No hay nada mejor que hacer el amor con el amor (There is nothing better than making love with love) and Benditas sábanas blancas (Blessed White Sheets). The first was born from seeing how couples destroy themselves, looking outside for what they already have at home. The second is understanding that many couples deprive themselves of enjoying intimacy simply due to sexual illiteracy, not knowing that their bodies are also a blessing.

I also had a deep academic dream: to reach the final step. The doctorate. Today, by the grace of God, that yearning is also being fulfilled. I am finalizing my PhD degree, as a testimony that pain does not stop you when faith is greater than fear.

Even the smallest fears, like driving on highways, were transformed. They used to paralyze me. Today, I feel like a Formula 1 driver. The fright left in the most miraculous way: as night leaves when the sun prevails.

Today I shout it loudly and with gratitude: This Claudia does not give up.

And I do not say it to exalt myself, but to give glory to the God who has restored, sustained, and lifted me every day of my life.

Let's Learn More About Claudia P. Álvarez

CLAUDIA PATRICIA ÁLVAREZ is a married woman and mother of two children, holding a Doctorate in Psychology and Sexology. She has walked in her Christian faith for over forty years. Currently, she congregates at the CCC Christian Community, where she continues to serve with love, conviction, and dedication. As a speaker and workshop facilitator, Claudia accompanies couples in processes of restoration and growth. She does this from a holistic perspective that unites psychological science and faith, promoting emotional, sexual, and spiritual completeness.

She is the author of several books, including "Benditas Sábanas Blancas," a work that was accepted as a doctoral thesis and published by JDN PUBLICATIONS. Today, she participates as a co-author of the book Entre Amigas: Historias del Alma que Inspiran e Impactan (Among Friends: Stories from the Soul that Inspire and Impact), reaffirming her commitment to inner healing, faith, and love that transform lives.

Claudia, a friend whom I admire, a warrior woman, and a

professional in everything she does, was one of the first people I met here in the city where I live when I first arrived. Together, we have worked for the community and contributed our grain of sand in different areas of leadership. Thank you for being such a blessing.

Among Friends

FIFTH
STORY

DIVINE LOVE
AND
PROTECTION"

Judian Bartolomey
New Bedford, MA

5

DIVINE LOVE AND PROTECTION
BY JUDIAN BARTOLOMEY, NEW BEDFORD, MA

From before my birth, God had me covered with His love and purpose. At age 12, my mother became pregnant. In her desperation, she considered aborting me. But God had a plan for me and preserved me in my mother's womb.

Now, as an adult, I better understand her situation. She was just a child, with an adult body but a young mind, facing difficult circumstances. My mother also carried deep wounds. When she was born, her own mother abandoned her in a box of bananas for someone to find.

But God sent a kind woman who rescued her, cared for her, and became her godmother. Looking at our history, I know that generational curses exist, but they can only be broken by seeking God, who transforms our lives.

My childhood was very difficult. My mother immigrated to the United States, and my sisters and I were left in the care of our great-grandmother, who, although not a Christian, still taught us good values. She used to say, "Where one person eats, ten can eat," and although there was scarcity, she always helped those in need, trusting that God would provide.

Despite moments of loneliness and abandonment, I found comfort in God. I used to ask myself, "Are You real?" because I desperately needed to feel a father's love. My refuge was my conversations with Him, writing to Him in a notebook while sitting behind the bathroom door. At age 10, I accepted Christ into my heart.

Although I faced opposition, I learned that prayer and fasting break chains and that God has more power than any adversity. God was my refuge and my strength when I faced scorn, abuse, and temptations in a difficult environment. He protected and guided me, as His word says in Psalm 46:1: "God is our refuge and strength, an ever-present help in trouble."

Despite living surrounded by harmful practices, I chose to follow Christ. Young people buying drugs would question why my family sold what I was advising them not to consume. I told them there was a better way, that they could change, because John 8:36 says:

"So if the Son sets you free, you are truly free."

The difficult times did not cease. There was extreme scarcity—so much so that my great-grandmother would cut one apple into 12 pieces to share among us. Our house burned down, and we had nothing. We took refuge where we could, but despite everything, God had a greater purpose.

In the midst of despair, I learned that trials do not last forever and that God is always working in our story. When I arrived in the United States at 17, arguments with my mother were constant. Until one day, on December 31st, I decided to pray to God with all my might, asking Him for peace between us. That same day, in the middle of an attempted argument, I told her, "I'm sorry, but I'm not going to fight with you anymore. The battle is not ours, but the Lord's." And God heard my prayer.

I understood that we should not focus on the enemy, but on God, because Romans 8:37 assures us: "In all these things we are more than conquerors through him who loved us."

Today I know that God is my refuge, my strength, and my best friend. I have learned to trust in Him at all times—in trials and in joy. His love never fails, and prayer connects us with the Father, the Son, and the Holy Spirit. Psalm 91:1-2 declares:

> *"He who dwells in the shelter of the Most High will abide in the shadow of the Almighty. I will say to the LORD, 'My refuge and my fortress, my God, in whom I trust.'"*

Trials come, but they do not last forever. God gives us the victory if we choose to put our faith in Him. I hope this version of your story faithfully reflects your testimony and God's love in your life. May the Lord continue to bless and guide you in His purpose.

"Today I can say with all my heart that my God is faithful. He has given me a beautiful family, a wonderful husband, and four children, with whom we walk hand-in-hand with God. If you have not yet taken the step of faith or do not know God, I hope my story helps you to know that if He could do it for me, He can do it for you too. Stop blaming yourself for your past; come to Him, for He has the solution to all your problems, questions, and anxieties. His love is real, and you can put your life in His hands so that the Holy Spirit may touch your heart, and you can have a personal relationship with Jesus.

As the Scripture says:

> *"Casting all your care upon Him, for He cares for you."*
> *(1 Peter 5:7)*

"Therefore, if anyone is in Christ, he is a new creation; old things have passed away; behold, all things have become new." (2 Corinthians 5:17)

Let's Learn More About Judian Bartolomey

JUDIAN IS an example of resilience and dedication to her home, her husband, and her children. Always willing to serve, she has been a great support to various ministries and her local church, including valuable support to the Entre Amigas International Ministry. In fact, she traveled with us to Colombia when we took Entre Amigas to Monte Líbano, and she joined our ministry when we celebrated Entre Amigas in Taunton, MA.

Judian, thank you for your powerful testimony that reveals God's purpose in life and His unbreakable divine protection. We hope this opportunity encourages you to write more; it is clear that when God has a purpose for someone, He cares for them diligently. Thank you for your valuable contribution to this book by sharing your story with us. Go forward in the Lord!

Erica V. Figueroa
Dartmouth, MA

SIXTH
STORY

FEELINGS OF MATERNAL HELPLESSNESS AND HOW TO OVERCOME IT

6

FEELING OF MATERNAL HELPLESSNESS, AND HOW TO OVERCOME IT

BY ERICA V. FIGUEROA, DARTMOUTH, MA

I would like to begin by defining the term "impotence." According to the Royal Spanish Academy, it refers to the lack of power or ability to accomplish something. The term can also be associated with the impossibility or incapacity to carry out an action.

When we link it to a concept as profound as motherhood, "maternal impotence" can be understood as the inability or impossibility to fully exercise the responsibilities of a mother, or the lack of power to change the circumstances, challenges, and difficulties that accompany this work.

Upon closely analyzing the topic I present, I was able to define it as that deep, internal struggle a mother faces when, despite her unconditional love and tireless efforts, there are situations that she simply cannot change with her own strength. This is a feeling that many mothers face at different times in their lives when, despite their love and dedication, circumstances escape their control and prevent them from offering what they would wish or what their children need.

Maternal impotence has nothing to do with a lack of responsibility, but with the profound emotional complexity that motherhood entails. It is that accumulation of immense love, unwavering commitment, and external circumstances that, at times, are beyond a mother's control, generating a feeling of helplessness.

I tell you that from the moment I first held my children in my arms, their arrival illuminated my heart with an indescribable joy, a delight that seemed to overflow with every heartbeat. I celebrated every stage of their growth, treasuring the moments of happiness and bravely facing those in which tears were inevitable. It was on that journey that I understood, in all its depth, the true meaning of Maternal love.

I always knew the day would come when they would set out on their own path, exploring new avenues in life. Together we dreamed big and faced challenges that seemed insurmountable. There were times of scarcity, hunger, and uncertainty in an unstable home.

These were difficult trials, but deep within my being, there was a strength that always drove me to protect, shelter, and guide my children with the purest and most unwavering love.

However, within that determined strength, an internal battle also exists: "impotence" or "powerlessness." That feeling that, at times, weakens us and makes us question every step, every decision we make in raising our children. We fight against our own doubts, against the fear of not doing enough, of not doing it well. And, as if that weren't enough, we must confront the relentless giant of "What will people say," that shadow that pursues us and compels us to overanalyze our actions, wondering if we are truly fulfilling our role in the correct manner.

In the moments when maternal powerlessness invades us, when we feel that our strength is insufficient and that circumstances escape our control, that is when we must turn to someone greater, to a refuge that offers us peace and direction.

In my case, that refuge is God, sovereign and powerful, who not only cares for my children but also grants me the wisdom to guide them with love and purpose.

He gives us the tools to cultivate in them the capacity to make discerning decisions—decisions that lead them, first and foremost, to a life pleasing to God, but also to a healthy existence in all aspects. Not a perfect life, because perfection is unattainable, but a stable life that allows them to face challenges with firmness and enjoy a true quality of life.

We are accustomed to hearing "motherhood is a path without manuals," but it is a role we assume with love, which often comes with uncertainty. We prepare ourselves to nurture, educate, and protect our children, but we are never fully ready for the unexpected challenges that may arise. What should we do when a child's rebellion becomes a dominant factor at home? When our children face internal battles with their mental health, or struggle with disabilities or physical limitations? How do we handle the pain of seeing them fall into self-destruction through drugs, alcohol, or harmful relationships?

And even more heartbreaking, how do we comfort a child who faces a great battle with their identity every day, who cannot bear the reflection they see in the mirror, who clings to their flaws and fails to recognize their own light? How do we respond to the enormous demands that life imposes on them, and on us as mothers?

A mother who takes shelter under the shadow of the Almighty feels secure; she finds true wisdom. God is the guide who illuminates her understanding and provides the right words to help our children discover their identity in Him. When a mother seeks refuge in God, she develops a greater wisdom, capable of teaching them to love themselves, because she herself has understood that God loved us first. This gives her the capacity to comprehend the infinite love that God has for humanity, steering them away from self-destruction and leading them toward a place of self-love and acceptance, as unique beings created by God.

We have been called to overcome the silent pain—I speak of the pain of wanting to protect, heal, guide, or save a child, but feeling that circumstances are beyond our control. It is a weight that oppresses the heart. Amidst this, I have striven to maintain a hope that never extinguishes: The longing to see a child free from the vice of drugs, from that which has deceived their mind, chaining them to a dependence that has anesthetized their being. They no longer see their own greatness, their purpose, their light. For the mother who faces this battle day after day, powerlessness can consume her. The physical, mental, and spiritual toll is profound, for in her unwavering love she tries, with all her might, to break the vicious cycles that imprison her son or daughter. But when human strength is insufficient, when strategies fail, and the heart falters, the only true refuge is God.

The Bible, the word of God, gives us a moving example in the story of Hagar and her son Ishmael, showing us the heart of a mother who, in her anguish, had to watch her son suffer from afar under the threat of a dangerous environment resulting from the temperatures and scarcity in the desert. In her despair, she cried out to God, and He answered, rescuing Ishmael and assuring him a promising future. This is a reminder that, even when we see our children face challenges and dangers, God is always present, observing every circumstance and extending His hand of salvation, bringing peace to a mother's heart.

The word of God also tells us about the widow of Zarephath, who, in a moment of desperation and scarcity, faced the helplessness of not having enough to feed her son, feeling the great weight of uncertainty about how she would confront these circumstances. However, this woman trusted in God and, by obeying His word through the prophet Elijah, she witnessed the miracle of provision in her home. But the trial did not end there. When her son became gravely ill and died, her heart was filled with pain and anguish, unable to do anything to save him. Nevertheless, upon crying out to God, she witnessed the greatest restoration: her son was resurrected.

The stories of these two mothers show us that, no matter how overwhelming the despair may be, God always extends His hand. They found in Him strength and provision to move forward, and in the same way, you, mother reading this, can overcome the challenge of powerlessness every day. You are not alone in this battle; together, we will conquer it with firm steps in faith. Here are some examples of how we can overcome maternal powerlessness:

- Crying out to God in the midst of anguish, surrendering all pain, knowing that He listens and responds.
- Depending on His provision, trusting that He will sustain every need, because His faithfulness is unwavering.
- Not allowing fear to conquer us, because fear paralyzes, but faith compels us to trust in the divine purpose for our children. The perfect love of God casts out fear.
- Maintaining the character of Christ, cultivating love, patience, and temperance to guide them with wisdom, even in the most difficult moments.
- Standing firm in self-control when circumstances often shake us and lead us into emotional chaos.
- Awaiting hope in God, clinging to the certainty that He has the power to transform, heal, and restore our children, even when all seems lost.

Dare to face the challenges, embrace every stage in the trajectory of being a mother, and remember that it is not about being a perfect mother, but about being a present mother who trusts in God's faithfulness and reflects God's character even in the most difficult circumstances.

By Erica V. Figueroa

Learn more about Erica V. Figueroa

ERICA V. Figueroa was born in Villalba, Puerto Rico, on April 16, 1975. She spent her adolescence in Coto Laurel, Ponce, Puerto Rico, and completed part of her secondary education in Rochester, New York. In 2011, she earned her **Bachelor's Degree in Pedagogy** from the Interamerican University of Puerto Rico. As a believer, she attended the Bible Institute in Massachusetts as part of her ministerial formation. She currently resides in Dartmouth, Massachusetts, with her husband, José.

Erica has a distinguished career in **social work and family support**. She worked for five years with vulnerable families as a home visitor in the Early Head Start program. For the past nine years, she has served as a **mental health social worker** for children and adolescents with emotional disorders. She is an active member of the Crown of Life Church, INC. in Fall River, Massachusetts, and a faithful believer in the Gospel of Christ. Her hobbies include reading, enjoying her pets, nature walks, and spending time with her grandchildren.

Motivated by her **literary dream**, Erica contacted JDN, who encouraged and advised her, recognizing the potential of her story. This is how she joined JDN and became an author, fulfilling her goal with her first book, *"Me Tocó Vivir"* (I Had To Live), published by JDN PUBLICATIONS.

SEVENTH
STORY

I SURVIVED

Nilsa M. Ortiz
Providence, RI

I SURVIVED

BY NILSA MINELLYS ORTIZ, PROVIDENCE, RI

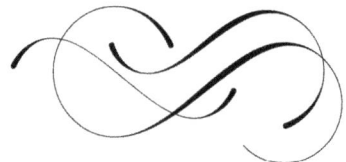

I got married full of hopes, and what began as a dream collapsed in the blink of an eye. It's a feeling similar to holding something immensely valuable and fragile in your hands, only to have an overwhelming wind knock it down and shatter it into a thousand pieces. The door opened, and with it, violence entered: not only physical but also emotional, economic, and psychological.

It was an extremely difficult time. I had only been in that place for a short time, with no friends or family. I felt alone, scared, angry, and full of frustration. My broken pride screamed the loudest, and a deep fear had gripped my soul; I trembled just hearing his voice.

One night, while I was sleeping, I felt a dark, malevolent weight on me. His hands wrapped around my neck, and the air began to escape my body. My mind, clouded and confused, struggled incessantly. I could only think of my daughter: "Will I ever see her again? What will become of her? Who will protect her? She needs me, she is so small." As the air left without return and my lungs emptied, I passed out.

At that moment, I thought luck was on my side, as I was far from God and couldn't see His saving hand. "I married to serve Him, and now His servant is abusing me?" I wondered. No one would believe me. He was "the man of God," and I was the newcomer to a congregation where no one knew me.

In that battle, he believed he had won. He left me there, sprawled, breathless, presuming I was dead. But in some miraculous way, a thread of air slipped into my aching lungs, and I could breathe again. I cried intensely and rushed to see my little girl. She was asleep, unaware of anything. Thank God for that. I wanted to run away nonstop, to leave everything behind, but where? With whom?

It was complete uncertainty. At that time, I didn't even feel capable of taking care of my daughter. I couldn't tell my family, who were so far away. I always felt guilt, and I believed my family would blame me and point fingers at me for being a "bad mother" and a "bad woman." I felt dirty, fragile, and without strength, just like during the times he sexually assaulted me. I feared he would return to attack me again.

When he arrived from work, as if nothing had happened, my entire being trembled. He brought me flowers, chocolates, and food. I summoned the courage to survive a few more days while I planned how to escape. There was nothing that could stop me from leaving that place where I had been so utterly violated in every sense.

With the help of a local agency dedicated to assisting victims of domestic violence, I took what I could and left that house for a place where he would never find me. God hid me in His hands, and he has not found me to this day. I have reconciled and fallen in love with my God again.

Learn more about Nilsa M. Ortiz

NILSA MADE her debut as a writer by sharing her powerful testimony in the book "El Silencio No Funciona"(Silence Doesn't Work), published by Edna L. Isaac and Elizabeth Puello of JDN, a work that directly addresses domestic violence. If you wish to read her story, she shares how she survived two tough trials and moved forward.

Today, that tragedy has become a transformative advantage. Nilsa dedicates her life to helping women and individuals going through various difficult situations, working as a Community Mental Health Agent.

Thank you, Nilsa, for sharing your heart with us again and for your service to the community.

EIGHTH
STORY

THE TRAINING

ELIZABETH WALCOTT
CHICAGO, IL

8

THE TRAINING

BY ELIZABETH WALCOTT, CHICAGO, IL

Training is a fundamental foundation for every Christian. Jesus Himself dedicated time to training His disciples about the Kingdom of light and the kingdom of darkness. Every created element has an origin, and the world, though it has a beginning, is heading toward an end or a restoration. The believer, one who identifies as a Christian, needs to be continuously trained by the Holy Spirit.

Ministerial mission is another vital part of our existence. Every church is established with a divine purpose. The question is: What is yours? Every human being created by God possesses a unique purpose. The ministerial calling is merely the beginning of the mission God entrusts to you here on Earth, using you as His instrument. There are corporate missions (of the church as a body) and a personal mission. But what is yours? After God imparts His gifts to you and calls you, what more needs to be done?

The real training begins when you surrender your life to Jesus. The miracles of the past are only a manifestation of God's power. However, the manifestations of the church as a unified entity are of regional and global scope, and have a spontaneous and perpetual influence. This means that if your church is building up only internally, are you only impacting those inside? Where are your missionaries? Where are your evangelists? Ministries must be supported and educated to transcend the four walls of the temple, continuously, so that the power of God may be fully manifested. As a pastor, it is your duty to support those brothers and sisters who are missionaries or evangelists, so that the Church of Christ continues to grow. Current Western civilization has created a local mentality, focused only on impact at the pastoral and episcopal ministry level. But what about the other ministries and gifts?

Every person has a main calling: to carry the Gospel to all nations. Beyond being a pastor, what is your personal calling in this Great Commission given to all of us? It is not that you should leave the pastorate, but that the Great Commission is for each one of us. Are you living that out?

What is the Father's vision for your life? What is the Father's mission pertinent to you? Are we fulfilling it?

Since when have we stopped growing in God's spiritual gifts? Today, the Lord placed it on my heart to minister about our love for Him. It is not about ministry or gifts, but about loving Him more than all things; about spending time with Him, about falling more in love with the Holy Spirit.

While we were praying, we felt we should prolong our prayer time because we touched on a crucial theme: time with God and making Him the most important thing to us. Fall more in love with spending time in His presence.

I want to share something with you that I believe is very important and essential for all children of God.

He (Jehovah) Said It and He Did It

When man and woman sinned in Eden, God told the woman that her seed would bruise the enemy's head and that the serpent would bruise his heel, and so it was! When God spoke to Moses about bringing His people out of Egypt and giving them a land flowing with milk and honey, so it was! When God told Joshua that he would take the land and that the walls of Jericho would fall so that His people would possess the land, so it was! The prophet Isaiah prophesied about our Savior and what His crucifixion would be like, and so it was! Jesus told His disciples that He would send the Holy Spirit after departing from them, and so it was! Jesus also told us that He is coming again, and so it will be!

Everything God has spoken through His prophets has been fulfilled. Not a jot or tittle will pass. What God said will happen and we will see it with our own eyes. Therefore, who am I to doubt what God has already said He is going to do with me (with you)? We were born to continue God's mandate here on Earth. The Father's mission will be fulfilled, and you will be an instrument in the hands of Jehovah to plant, pull down, and destroy the works of the enemy.

When you see and feel a lot of opposition, remember that you have within you the One who said "let there be" and so it was. He never lies. God has not made a mistake with you. Great battles are given to those who know how to resist. The one who resists becomes stronger; when you resist, you build strength and develop more powerful spiritual muscles. God trusts you; He knows He can count on you. No matter the difficulty, God has equipped you to take, win, and conquer. Take the territories the Father has given you!

Hebrews 12:4 reminds us that, the more you resist, the more strength is created within your spiritual muscles.When you pray and feel like you can't go on, that is precisely when you need to pray the most, because you are at the breaking point, at the threshold of a manifestation.

God wants to reveal Himself more in you and use you, but He cannot if your muscles are weak. You need to create resistance by praying, reading the Word in meditation, resisting sin, laziness, and complacency. Immerse yourself more in His presence, create a place of altar where the fire of God is perceived, is felt, so that those around you say: "There is something special about you."

Trials are not forever. If you are in a trial that seems endless, then you need to resist so you can create those spiritual muscles and be like Paul, who, despite being in prison, was one of those who wrote the most in the New Testament. In your weakness and in your trial, God wants to glorify Himself. True transformation is seen when you are creating resistance. Do not stop at the moment your muscles are being trained and broken down. Do not stop in the middle of the training! "Resist!" Be strong in the power of His might. Keep praying until God begins to show you His will for you and the mission you have here on Earth.

Learn more about Elizabeth Walcott

A WOMAN PASSIONATE about God and His work, Elizabeth Walcott firmly believes that God's plan and design must be fulfilled in our lives, for souls increasingly need Him. This is her deep passion for God and souls. Her life has been guided by three fundamental pillars: her Creator, her family, and then everything else. Love for God is the most important thing to her.

When her daughter was born, she was married to a soldier in the military, who snatched away from her arms what she loved most after God: her daughter. In that instant, Elizabeth lost everything, including her possessions. But, being a woman who does not surrender, she felt a strength in her heart that whispered: "If he can be a soldier, so can you." Thus, she enlisted in the American military. From there, a new stage in her life began. At the same time, God opened doors for her to preach the Gospel in various nations, including Europe.

By God's grace and mercy, Elizabeth has served the Almighty for over 15 years. She has written projects and books, including "Entre 2 Mundos" (Between 2 Worlds) published by JDN PUBLI-

CATIONS, which was also published in English. She has been trained by the earthly military and by the military of the Kingdom of Jesus Christ. By His grace, today she is the owner of non-profit and for-profit organizations, including her first FM Radio 105.5 "Jesus Para las Naciones" (Jesus For the Nations), located in Illinois. She is also the CEO of the JFTN-JLPN ministry (Jesus for the Nations - Jesús Para las Naciones), through which she carries the Kingdom of Christ with conferences, studies, and campaigns. Everything has been due to the Father's love and mercy towards her. To Jehovah be the Glory!

Elizabeth Puello
New Jersey, USA

NINTH
STORY

WHAT IF EVERYONE LEAVES AND I'M LEFT WITHOUT FRIENDS?

9

WHAT IF EVERYONE LEAVES, AND I'M LEFT WITHOUT FRIENDS?

BY ELIZABETH PUELLO, NEW JERSEY, US

"A friend loves at all times, and a brother is born for adversity." — Proverbs 17:17

A true friend loves you at all times, regardless of your condition or situation. When distress strikes, she stands by you, drawing near to support you in every need. A sister might get angry with you, but she will never stop being your sister. Even if she says, "I don't want you near me," a moment passes, and she already longs to share time with you—she misses you. And if something happens to her or someone offends her, she is the first to leap to your defense. I knew of a case where a young woman was upset with her brother; one day he suffered an accident, and she couldn't stop crying for him. That's what a friend is: like a sister, she loves at all times, no matter the circumstance.

Love is unconditional and eternal. It is a decision: you choose whether or not to love. However, according to the Word of God, we must love everyone equally, even our enemies. A friend, even if long periods pass without seeing each other, welcomes you with affection, without asking why you haven't sought her out or called. She simply enjoys your company. True love should never end; if it is genuine, it remains forever, as the Bible says: *"Love never fails."*

It strikes me deeply that Jesus, even when being sold by Judas, called him "friend." This made me understand that Jesus's love and friendship for Judas were unconditional. Jesus continued to call Judas a friend, even knowing that he would betray Him. Judas did not honor his title as a friend; he betrayed Jesus.

A friend's love should be like that love the Bible speaks of: a true love that provides you with security and trust, and that is unconditional.

What is the love the Bible refers to?

Love is patient, love is kind. It does not envy, it does not boast, it is not proud. It does not dishonor others, it is not self-seeking, it is not easily angered, it keeps no record of wrongs. Love does not delight in evil but rejoices with the truth. It always protects, always trusts, always hopes, always perseveres. 1 Corinthians 13:4-7 (New International Version)

A friend who loves you is patient with you when you don't understand something, when you feel confused or lost, or when you are wrong. A friend who loves you will always tend to do good to you; she will never want to harm you. She will not show jealousy over your projects or pride when asking for and granting forgiveness. She is kind, sincere, supports you in your decisions, does not envy your achievements, corrects you, and even as time passes, she always welcomes you the same way. When she doesn't have an answer to your problem, she prays for you. She does not judge you, she does not criticize you to others, but she corrects you when necessary and does not embarrass you in front of others.

That kind of friend seems difficult to find, but in God, it is possible. A friend is a refreshment, an outlet when you have had a bad day. She is patient when you don't want to talk, she lends you her ears without interrupting, and she accompanies you in prayer in times of need.

Some Examples of True Friendship:

The Example of David and Jonathan (1 Samuel 20:17-18):

THIS IS a great example of true friendship. They had a friendship that they respected above adversity, despite the fact that Saul, Jonathan's father, wanted to kill David. Jonathan was faithful to David more than a brother, defending him even from his own father, and demonstrating his love. Likewise, David honored their friendship by honoring Jonathan's family. When David became king, he did not forget his friend's family. A friend will honor you even after you are gone. He or she will not expose your flaws to others, and will speak well of you even in your absence. Your friend will feel like she is talking about her life when she talks about you.

The Example of Ruth and Naomi (Ruth 1:16-17):

"But Ruth replied, 'Don't urge me to leave you or to turn back from you. Where you go I will go, and where you stay I will stay. Your people will be my people and your God my God. Where you die I will die, and there I will be buried. May the Lord deal with me, be it ever so severely, if even death separates you and me.'"

After the death of Ruth's husband, Naomi had no obligation to her, but Ruth decided to be her friend regardless of whether or not she would have descendants. This was such a great display of love that today Ruth is honored by God by appearing in the genealogy of Jesus. This means that God is pleased by sincere and loving friendship; He honors those who honor others.

Abraham was called a friend of God:

"But you, Israel, my servant, Jacob, whom I have chosen, you descendants of Abraham my friend."

How wonderful it is to be called a friend of God! Abraham led a life that honored God with his faith, listened to Him when He spoke, and obeyed Him in everything, even to the point of daring to offer his son as a sacrifice. That sacrifice did not take place physically, but it did in the spiritual world and in Abraham's heart; he decided wholeheartedly to make the sacrifice, as the most important thing was not the child, but doing God's will and being obedient. This is how we must have God first in our lives; that our happiness or fulfillment is not in what we have received from Him, but in Him Himself, in the Holy Spirit, our best friend.

What if everyone leaves, and I am left without friends?

Loneliness can make you feel empty and sad. No one likes to be alone, but there are times when everyone distances themselves, no one takes your calls, and it seems as if you are invisible at gatherings.

I want to tell you that this loneliness is not external, but internal. A person can be surrounded by many people and still feel lonely. It seems paradoxical, but when you feel lonely, others tend to distance themselves even more, and when you feel accompanied and enjoy yourself, everyone wants to be with you. There is a body and gestural language; you can communicate your state of mind without saying a word. It happens that others perceive you just as you feel internally: your eyes, your gaze, your face, and even your body posture reveal your emotional state. Therefore, it is necessary to feel accompanied from within. How is that achieved? By ensuring that your feeling of being accompanied and happy does not depend on those around you, that happiness is your inner essence, without waiting for someone to come and make you laugh.

Even if everyone leaves, don't feel alone. Remember that the One who created you has never left you and never will."The Lord is my shepherd, I lack nothing," as the Psalmist David said in Psalm 23.

The Holy Spirit is your best friend

We must know who the Holy Spirit is. He is the one whom Jesus left as our Comforter. He fills every void, makes loneliness flee, listens to you, understands you, strengthens you, and guides you in all your paths if you ask Him and allow Him.

The Holy Spirit is the one who reminds us of everything Jesus has told us in His word, John 14:26:

> *"But the Advocate, the Holy Spirit, whom the Father will send in my name, will teach you all things and will remind you of everything I have said to you."*

To get the Holy Spirit to remind us of what Jesus said, we must read the Bible, meditate on it, and put it into practice in daily life. The best way to hear God's voice is through His Word.

If I have the Holy Spirit, His fruit is manifested in me. The Bible speaks of the fruit of the Spirit in the apostle Paul's letter to the Galatians:

> *"But the fruit of the Spirit is love, joy, peace, forbearance, kindness, goodness, faithfulness, gentleness and self-control. Against such things there is no law."*

How can I have a life of intimacy with my friend, the Holy Spirit? By trusting Him, casting your anxieties upon Him, reading the Word, fasting, praying, talking with Him as what He is: a person. You will never feel lonely with His company.

Put away all bitterness

One of the things that causes bitterness is contempt, but you must not allow that pain to turn into bitterness. You are not a gold coin to be liked by everyone; many will like you, but others will not want to see you, even in photographs. When they speak of you contemptuously or to criticize you, pay them no attention, do not swallow that poison, do not let that poison reach your heart so that it does not turn into pain. If you swallow it and it reaches your heart, it will turn into bitterness, and this will be like an infected wound that produces resentment and unforgiveness.

If resentment has already entered your heart, there is still an opportunity for healing. We must forgive immediately not to distance ourselves from our friend, the Holy Spirit. The Bible rightly says: "If I do not forgive my sister or friend, my Father who is in heaven will not forgive me."

Do nothing that grieves the Holy Spirit. Always maintain firm obedience. When you are going to do something, first consider if it is in accordance with the Word of God and if it will not drive away your best friend. Maintain a constant relationship with the Holy Spirit. He is your best friend; you will never feel alone with Him by your side.

Learn more about Elizabeth Puello

ELIZABETH PUELLO WAS BORN in the Dominican Republic in a town called Bonao, the daughter of Pelgio Puello and Lina Rodríguez. She is married to Aurelio Cornielle Arias, with whom she has three children. She completed her studies at the Autonomous University of Santo Domingo, where she earned a Bachelor's Degree in Clinical Psychology, a Bachelor's Degree in School Psychology, a Master's Degree in Family Therapy, and several diplomas in different areas of Mental Health. She worked for several years as a psychologist at Villa Duarte municipal hospital in Santo Domingo and as a learning therapist in several educational centers. She also worked as a therapist and professor of psychology and guidance at the Instituto Técnico Superior Comunitario (ITSC), and is currently a writer and speaker, preaching the word of God so that souls may be saved. Among her published books are: Resiliencia (Resilience), Perdón a Través de la Acción (Forgiveness Through Action), Disciplinando con Amor (Disciplining with Love), and Mujeres Resilientes de fe Cristiana

(Resilient Women of Christian Faith), with JDN PUBLICATIONS. She is now a co-author of Entre Amigas, Historias del Alma Que Inspiran e Impactan (Among Friends, Stories of the Soul That Inspire and Impact).

TENTH
STORY

GROWING UP IN A DYSFUNCTIONAL FAMILY

JENNY FORTES
NEW BEDFORD, MA

10

GROWING UP IN A DYSFUNCTIONAL FAMILY

BY PASTOR JENNY FORTES, NEW BEDFORD, MA

Greetings, I am Pastor Jenny Fortes. Through this humble servant, I will share part of my story, and I declare, in the name of Jesus, that it will be a blessing to your lives.

I come from divorced parents and grew up in a dysfunctional family. My biological father had multiple relationships and even children outside the home. When he returned, he physically abused and mistreated my mother.

My mother decided to flee to Puerto Rico so he would no longer know of her whereabouts, thus keeping us safe. Although she was already a professional accountant and a university graduate, as a single mother with two children, she struggled to finish her academic preparation and get ahead.

I grew up admiring her bravery and determination. She didn't need her husband because, even without knowing God, He gave her the strength and had placed a vision in her: to return to her homeland, Puerto Rico, to build a home for herself and her two children.

From my mother, I learned the meaning of bravery: a heroic

deed or feat executed with courage. To me, she was my heroine. Physically, bravery allows us to overcome fears, and I imagine she was full of them. Alone with two small children, she had to work to feed three mouths—yes, three!—because our little poodle, Fifí, completed the trio.

I speak fear and admiration, and now I will tell you why. I remember that at age 9, already on the island, my biological father showed up at our door. Every child wants to see their parents happy and together, but this was not my case. My mother could not believe her eyes. How could this man reach Puerto Rico without speaking Spanish, when in the neighborhoods you get around by landmarks? He arrived in a carro público, a taxi, because his obsession with my mother was immense.

My parents began to argue. My father took her to the bathroom, and the argument continued. Suddenly, we heard nothing, and my mom didn't come out. My brother, who was older than me, always took the initiative. We agreed to break down the bathroom door with a machete my mom kept. Upon opening it and pulling back the curtain, we saw him strangling my mother by the neck. He was 6'1" and my mother 5'3".

When he saw us, he released my mother, grabbed my brother by the neck, and took him to the balcony. I remember starting to scream at him: "Let him go, Daddy, let him go!" My mind always goes back to that last word: "Let him go."

My mother experienced things that must have been horrible at the time, but without her even understanding anything about God yet, He protected her from that man who suffered from mental disorders. Mental illnesses are real. They were difficult to detect before, but today, with the advancement of science, it is easier to diagnose them, and many organizations can help. My biological father had deserted the Navy; he had fled and did not complete his service. Years later, when I was already an adult, my mom told me that one day my father sat her on the bed and began playing

Russian roulette with his pistol pointed at her head. While recounting this story, or rather, this horrible experience, she was still trembling, and her eyes reflected the terror. Poor my mother, how much she suffered at the hands of that man.

In time, my stepfather appeared, and I understood that he came to heal the wounds caused by an abusive man. God will send someone to help you heal. Years later she told me she felt a burden lift from her shoulders when he arrived. She would no longer be alone.

This man was exemplary, compassionate, loving, and humble. A man from a good family, with very traditional beliefs and strong religious values. He loved her and her two children. Years later, I managed to lead my mother to Christ. She began to persevere alongside my stepfather, and in 2010, they were both baptized in the Christian Church of Pastor Joanne Soto in Barceloneta, Puerto Rico.

God worked with her, but He also equipped the person who found her in pieces. That man was a "safe place" for her. God sent a man with all the tools to help her heal emotionally and mentally. Healing emotional wounds takes time; it is an individual process where you must allow your mind and body to work at their own pace. God healed every wound in her heart.

What did I learn from my mother? I learned to be a fighter, not to give up, and not to accept "you can't do that." Even before she knew God, He was already enabling her to be an instrument and channel of blessing so that we would understand the concept of "I can do all things through Christ who strengthens me" and never give up, no matter how difficult the situation was.

On January 9, 2014, God called her to His presence. Now she will receive her eternal reward.

Learn more about Jenny Fortes

JENNY FORTES' vision is to leave a legacy that impacts the community in the genuine transformation of the Soul, Body, and Spirit, with Christ as the center and foundation of lives.

Jenny Fortes was born in New Bedford, Massachusetts, July 29, 1972. She was raised in the United States until age nine. Following her parents' divorce, she moved to Puerto Rico. Her mother was Puerto Rican, and her biological father was from Massachusetts. Adjusting to the island was initially difficult due to the language and cultural differences. She graduated from high school at Fernando Callejo High School in Manatí, Puerto Rico. While studying, Jenny worked in the afternoons at a shoe store. Later, she obtained a Certification as a chemical operator and worked for eight years at Pfizer Pharmaceuticals in Barceloneta, Puerto Rico, through temporary agencies.

She then moved to Florida, where she studied Criminal Justice at the Metropolitan University. Eventually, she returned to Massachusetts as an adult to provide medical care for her son. Jenny currently works as a Health Educator for the YWCA. Since childhood, she witnessed the mistreatment of women in different homes, including her own and that of a loved one. From this experience and her work at the YWCA, her passion and desire to help abused and mistreated women with low self-esteem emerged. From this calling, the Jehovah-Rapha Ministry was born—a ministry focused on restoring, raising up, and healing women.

Thank you, Pastor Jenny, for that testimony. Thank you for serving women who need healing and salvation.

ELEVENTH
STORY

WHEN EVERYTHING CHANGES, GOD REMAINS

Keren Sánchez
Boston, MA

11

WHEN EVERYTHING CHANGES, GOD REMAINS

BY KEREN SÁNCHEZ, BOSTON, MA

A Journey of Faith and Purpose

Have you ever felt lost amid a storm of change? Have you wondered whether you will find yourself again — whether God still sees you, whether your purpose still stands? In this writing, I will share how God helped me rediscover myself when I emigrated and experienced uprooting, transition, the pain of the unknown, and the loss of identity.

As a woman of faith, a mental health professional, and an empowerment coach, I faced not only the migratory process but also the inner silences: doubt, fear, the question, "Who am I now?" For years, I have accompanied families in their own struggles, but God also guided me to look inward, to write, to heal, and finally to give birth to Renace en la Tormenta(Reborn in the Storm), my first book.

In this account, I will testify about how I exchanged lies like "I am alone" or "I got lost along the way" for biblical truths: "The Lord will fight for you; you need only to be still" (Exodus 14:14), "God is our refuge and strength, an ever-present help in trouble"

(Psalm 46:1). I discovered that rebirth is not about going back to who you were before, but about embracing the woman transformed by the storm.

Each chapter of my book was a stage of spiritual reconstruction. Here, I will narrate part of that journey with real stories, devotional exercises, and intimate reflections that will help other women navigate their own changes, with the certainty that they are not alone.

My message is clear: if God began it, He would perfect it (Philippians 1:6). Because His faithfulness does not depend on where we are, but on the eternal purpose He placed in us. This story is for you, a woman leader, who in the midst of change chooses not to surrender, but to be reborn.

My story begins with a suitcase full of dreams and a mind clouded by fear. Like many women who emigrate, I felt lost. I left behind the known, the secure, my roots... and at times I also felt like I left pieces of myself. I thought: "I am no longer the same," "I have become disconnected from who I am." But it was precisely in the middle of that storm where God began a work of profound transformation in me.

What seemed like the end was only the beginning of a divine reconstruction. Every chapter of my life began to be rewritten by His hand. And that is how Renace en la Tormenta was born, my book, where I share how God helped me turn lies into truths, fear into faith, and pain into purpose.

I clung to promises like:

> *"Before I formed you in the womb I knew you, and before you were born I consecrated you"* (Jeremiah 1:5).
> *"The Lord will fulfill his purpose for me"* (Psalm 138:8).
> *"The one who calls you is faithful, and he will do it"* (1 Thessalonians 5:24).

During my transition, I learned that identity does not depend on a place, a culture, or a social position, but on the One who calls me His own from eternity. What I thought was a loss—my land, my networks, my stability—was actually a divine invitation to discover who I am beyond all of that. Uprooting, far from canceling my purpose, refined it. It stripped me of masks, titles, and external expectations, to show me that the eternal in me does not move, even if everything around me changes.

I discovered that God did not lose me along the way. Rather, he was waiting for me there. In the silent night of my uncertainty, in the solitary tears that no one saw, in the days where everything was new and overwhelming... He was there. His presence became closer than ever, and His Word more alive than my fears. I was not abandoned; I was sustained. I was not forgotten; I was transformed.

I reconnected with Him in ways so profound that I never imagined. And in that encounter, I rediscovered myself: loved, chosen, sent. I realized my transition was part of a greater plan to bless others. What seemed like the end of a story was merely the prologue to a full life, guided by grace.

My testimony is not just a personal story; it is a call. It is for you, brave woman, who in the middle of a transition felt that change broke you. It is for you who, when leaving behind a stage, a land, a dream, or a relationship, believed you were also leaving a part of yourself... perhaps the best part. It is for you who looked in the mirror and did not recognize your reflection, because your voice was silenced, your strength was gone, and hope became a distant whisper.

But today I come to remind you of something eternal: "You are in process; you are not lost." God is not finished with you. Even if you feel that everything is crumbling, He is rebuilding something firmer and more beautiful from the rubble. You are not alone, you are not broken without purpose, you are not a lost cause.

I speak to you from the cracks that are now healing with light. From the tears that watered a new faith. From a heart that was restored in the Potter's workshop. And with the same authority with which I lived it, today I tell you:

> "You are in the Master's hands. He who began a good work in you will carry it on to completion until the day of Christ Jesus" *(Philippians 1:6, NIV).*

No matter how much you have lost, what God is about to do in you will surpass everything that was left behind. Your story does not end in the storm... it begins in the rebirth.

This manuscript is not just a story; it is much more than words on paper. It is a brave invitation to be reborn, to discover the truth of who you are in Christ, and to hold on to the certainty that a storm cannot define your destiny. Sometimes life breaks everything we knew: a home, a routine, a dream, or even our own voice. But right there, at the epicenter of change, God can make room for a profound rebirth.

Imagine this: a woman who, with tears in her eyes, was picking up pieces of her lost past. She felt that everything was fading away... until she began to see that the loving hand of God was gathering every fragment. In the midst of chaos and uncertainty, that inner voice began to tell her: "Do not fade away, My daughter, I am creating something new and eternal in you." With each chapter, I accompany you on that real journey: from the move, the fear of the unknown, the longing for what was... to the resurgence of a powerful identity under your Father's grace.

If God did it with me, He can also do it with you. The same Creator who started working within you will not stop before carrying out His purpose. He does not change His plans, His love, or His presence. So, as you explore these pages, allow yourself to believe that you are in the faithful hands of the One who promises to complete what He started in you (Philippians 1:6). Because in every trial, there is a seed of grace. In every pain, there is ground for flourishing. In every farewell, there is a new beginning.

Five Questions to Reflect and Go Deeper

1. What "storm" do you have today that threatens to redefine you? How could you see it as ground for rebirth?
2. Where have you lost your voice or your purpose, and what revelation do you need to recover both?
3. What fragment of your past do you need to surrender to God so that He can reconstruct it into greatness?
4. How does the promise that He will perfect the work He began in you manifest in your life (Philippians 1:6)?
5. What step of faith are you called to take today to declare that you believe in your own inner resurrection?

Continue going deeper with the book, *Renace en la Tormenta.*
Accompany yourself with devotionals, exclusive content, and mentorship on my platforms. Join the Academy of Transformation and continue growing alongside other women of faith: https://kerensanchez.com/academia-atmai/ Your process is just beginning. And you are not alone! I am here to accompany you. Social Media Instagram: https://www.instagram.com/kerensanchezcoach Facebook: https://www.facebook.com/kerensanchezcoach

Learn more about Keren Sánchez

KEREN SÁNCHEZ IS AN AUTHOR, pastor, worshiper, and mentor of Christian women, with a passionate voice for spiritual empowerment. Author of the book Renace en la Tormenta, her story of emigration, faith, and restoration has inspired hundreds of women to rediscover their purpose amidst life's most challenging changes.

With a Bachelor's degree in Accounting and Administration, a specialization in Human Resources Management, and a Master's degree in Human Services, Keren has complemented her academic training with certifications in Christian Life Coaching, Transformational Mentorship, and various certifications in the field of professional development. She is currently pursuing a Master's degree in Mental Health and Psychology.

This preparation has allowed her to guide other women with excellence, integrating professional knowledge with the direction of the Holy Spirit.

As a pastor and worshiper, she ministers not only with her words but also from the altar, carrying a message of restoration, identity, and fulfillment. She is the founder and director of the Academy of Transformation for the High-Impact Woman (Academia de Transformación para la Mujer de Alto Impacto), where she leads processes of healing and empowerment for women leaders who wish to heal their roots, embrace their divine design, and walk with purpose.

Additionally, she directs the group "Extraordinary Women with Purpose and in Victory" (Mujeres Extraordinarias con Propósito y en Victoria), a community where she daily inspires women to live by faith, guiding them in their spiritual growth, personal development, and the fulfillment of God's calling for their lives.

Her calling is clear: to help others be reborn from pain, recognizing that even in the midst of the storm, God is still working. Her message is an invitation to remember who we are in Christ, heal deep wounds, and embrace a new beginning with faith. She lives grateful for the grace of God that sustains her and sends her to lift up many more.

Among Friends

TWELFTH STORY

Acepting His Will

Dorothy Álvarez
República of Ecuador

12

ACCEPTING HIS WILL
PASTOR DOROTHY ÁLVAREZ, ECUADOR

I grew up in a Christian household. My parents taught me to love God, family and church. At the age of fourteen, I had personal experiences with God and decided that was what I wanted for my entire life. I sought to serve in all areas possible in the work. It was a very beautiful but also very difficult period of adolescence and youth because of the many circumstances I had to go through: trials, needs, temptations, and mistakes. However, I also have great memories, for God kept me and taught me to live for Him, without seeking the approval of men.

At nineteen, I met a missionary who came to preach in different cities in Ecuador. I didn't know that, seven years later, God would join our lives. I married at the age of twenty-six and went to live on the island of Aruba. Roberto, my husband, was a man of God—upright, wise, and very hardworking—prepared to lead a family. It was time to grow, and God sent us the best gifts: our three precious children were born: Benjamín, Joshua, and Sara.

We were a normal, happy family, but there was something that was always present in my husband's heart: the desire to serve God.

He always told me he had a deep calling to serve in Ecuador and shared his fervent longing to do missionary work in those remote places of the Ecuadorian Amazon. Honestly, I had become accustomed to a comfortable life and was against the idea of going as a missionary, because, in my mind, that meant suffering and experiencing want. I had seen many missionaries go through scarcity.

Until one day, during a fast, God spoke clearly to me that I should go with my husband to serve in Ecuador. I asked the Lord for one more sign: if He wanted us there, that someone would send us the tickets. That same night, someone called us from Ecuador and said, "I have your tickets, we await you in Ecuador." With that event, I surrendered everything that day and decided to join my husband's desire to preach in places where no one wanted to go.

So, in 2008, we left Aruba for a new city for us in the East (Oriente region). From the first day we arrived in that unknown city, the Lord showed us places to preach, focusing mainly on the indigenous people of the area. Doors began to open, and every week we visited different communities.

Also, in the city, we started a group in the living room of our house to gather people who needed God. We evangelized on the streets, and God added souls to His flock. It is true that it is beautiful to see what God does and how He restores lives, but at the same time, God had to process us and teach us to depend on Him absolutely. To learn, my husband, my three children, and I had to go through several moments of scarcity and need, which were necessary at that time so that the glory would be His alone.

Although the calling was being fulfilled, my husband had to fulfill a specific calling: to go to places where no one wants to go, where no one expects you, where you have to wait for them, where no one gives to you and you have to bring things to give, where no one praises you, and you receive rejection instead. But the calling must be fulfilled. Anyone who knows about this will understand that, for many, it is madness or a loss. However, the calling is like that: it must be fulfilled, because if it is not done, life will have no value or meaning for you.

Thus, my husband and I began to visit places no one wanted to visit—communities far from our comfort, five hours by car, two hours by boat, and often walking to be able to preach to people who eagerly waited for someone to visit them. Likewise, to carry out this evangelistic work, God took charge of providing all the necessary resources. And so several years passed in this work in the city and in different places, near and far.

In July 2023, my husband began to feel unwell. We thought the discomfort in his stomach was the result of indigestion. When we went to the doctor, after several tests, we received one piece of bad news after another and learned it was a terminal illness. And that's where another story begins. At that time, our children were living abroad, and we called them due to their father's serious condition.

Something to emphasize is that no one understands what is happening. Perhaps we thought: "It's a trial, God will heal him and perform a miracle so he can continue preaching the word. He has been a faithful man who has dedicated his whole life to doing God's work." Many arguments come to mind in those moments, as the will of God is not accepted. My children, always with their faith held high, said, "God will heal him," and we all held onto the hope of a miracle.

But as the days passed, my husband gathered the family and said:

"God has told me that He is going to take me. I want you to continue doing God's work. Don't be selfish; don't think only of yourselves. I am leaving happy because I did what God sent me to do; I feel satisfied."

During that period, his gifts were activated in a greater way, and he left a word from God for each of his children. He prayed for us, he blessed us, and those who came to visit him left comforted and with a word from God. God spoke to us through him, saying that his time had come and that we should accept His will.

It was not easy to describe what one feels in that moment, but what I can say is that even now we don't understand where such peace, strength, and comfort have come from. Only from God—there is no other explanation. A few days before his departure, he had not spoken for two days, but to say goodbye, he only sang a part of this worship song:

> "I am blessed, I live peacefully,
> I live in peace because God is always in control."

He departed with the Lord on September 7th. My three children and I continue the legacy he left us. We continue preaching, and we continue making trips to the jungle. I said "accepting His will," because for me, I still cannot believe that I am carrying on without him. My husband was the engine of everything, but now I understand that there is no one like God to heal, to sustain, to lift up, to console, and to strengthen.

There are moments of sadness, yes, we are human and normal, but my greatest refuge has been God. I find no other explanation than that He is the one who keeps me standing. To Him be the glory. No matter the pain, the trial, or the need we are going through. Today I can know that His Word is fulfilled and that we only depend on His mercy, and that His will is better than ours, even if we don't understand it.

Learn more about Dorothy Álvarez

DOROTHY GREW up in a Christian home where her parents transmitted the love of God, family, and the church to her. From her childhood, she had personal experiences with God that led her to dedicate her life to service. At twenty-six, she married and moved to the island of Aruba. God blessed her marriage with three children: Benjamín, Joshua, and Sara. Despite leading a comfortable life in Aruba, her husband felt a strong missionary calling toward the Ecuadorian Amazon. Initially, Dorothy resisted the idea, as she associated mission work with scarcity and suffering. She asked for a specific sign, and upon receiving immediate confirmation (the sending of plane tickets), in 2008, Dorothy gave up her former life to join the mission of preaching in remote places. They moved to a city in the East (Oriente region) of Ecuador, where the Lord guided them to preach, focusing primarily on the indigenous population. Her mission has centered on going to undesirable places, facing rejection, and taking the message to distant communities, accessible only after long journeys. Her husband departed with the Lord on September 7th;

however, Pastor Dorothy and her three children have taken on the commitment to continue the legacy, preaching and traveling to the jungle. She testifies that the peace, strength, and comfort that sustain her amidst the pain come solely from God, affirming that His will, though incomprehensible, is the best.

Thank you, Pastor Dorothy, for this great testimony where, despite the loss, the glory of God continues to shine and console.

Among Friends

THIRTEENTH STORY

WHAT HEAVEN CAN DO

Jeannett Toro
New Bedford, MA

13

WHAT HEAVEN CAN DO
PASTOR JEANNETT TORO, NEW BEDFORD, MA

"What is impossible with man is possible with God."
(Luke 18:27)

This story is not about theory, religion, or tradition, but about what heaven has worked for me. It is about the real and palpable power that comes from a living God. I am evidence that God still works miracles, that He still transforms, restores, and breathes life where everything seems dead.

I want to speak of what heaven can do, not as someone who repeats someone else's story, but as someone who has walked through the valley of the shadow of death and has been sustained by His hand. If you have ever felt insufficient, broken, abandoned, or without hope, this word is for you.

When I Thought I Was Incapable, God Called Me Capable

"But he said to me, 'My grace is sufficient for you, for my power is made perfect in weakness.'" (2 Corinthians 12:9)

I lived through moments when I didn't feel sufficient for what

God was asking of me. I doubted myself, my worth, and my gifts. The voice of insecurity shouted louder than my faith. But it was there that God looked at me with love and said: "Yes, you can, because I am with you." The fear didn't leave immediately, but His voice was stronger. He called me when I didn't feel worthy. He equipped me when I had no tools. He anointed me when I didn't even know how to speak. Heaven calls you for what He sees in you, not what you see today.

When I Was Betrayed by Man, God Was Faithful

> "Though my father and mother forsake me, the Lord will receive me." (Psalm 27:10)

One of the deepest wounds is betrayal. When you trust someone and they fail you, you feel your soul break. I lived it. My heart was pierced by unexpected words, actions, and decisions. But in the deepest darkness, I felt God's unwavering faithfulness. He sustained me when I no longer had strength. His love did not let me go for a day. His faithfulness taught me that even if man fails, He never changes. And this healed every broken corner.

When Doctors Said Having Children Was Impossible, God Gave Me an Inheritance

> "He grants the barren woman a home, like a joyful mother of children. Praise the Lord!" (Psalm 113:9)

Hearing I could not be a mother was a sentence that tore my soul. The medical reports were clear: there was no hope. But heaven had another plan. Against all odds, God gave me two natural daughters: Neyshali Anette Toro-Lacen and Nayeli Athalia

Toro. And not only that, but He has also given me many spiritual children.

Today I celebrate the life of my son-in-law, Derek Lacen, a gift from God to our family, and I embrace the blessing of being the wife of Neftalí Toro, a man transformed and raised as the priest of our home. Every life I can love and guide is part of the promise He made to me. Where science says "no," God says: "Yes, because I am the Creator of life."

When Everything Seemed Destroyed, God Made All Things New

"Behold, I make all things new." (Revelation 21:5)

I went through times when my life was in pieces. My home, my heart, my dreams... Everything seemed to collapse. But God told me, "I am making all things new." And He fulfilled it. He not only restored my heart but also transformed my husband, Neftalí Toro, into a man of honor, full of love; in short, a new man.

Seeing him love, serve, and walk with God is one of the most beautiful pieces of evidence of what heaven can do. Where you see ruins, God sees the foundation for something glorious.

When My Health Was at the Brink, God Breathed Life

"Then he said to me, 'Prophesy to the breath; prophesy, son of man, and say to it, "This is what the Sovereign Lord says: Come, breath, from the four winds and breathe into these slain, that they may live."'" (Ezekiel 37:9)

My body was affected by illness. The diagnoses were disheartening; I was told there wasn't much to be done. But, once again, heaven did not remain silent. God breathed life over me. I regained strength and purpose, and more than that: I understood that everything I experienced had a greater reason.

A Calling in the Midst of Pain

> *"You do not realize now what I am doing, but later you will understand." (John 13:7)*

In the middle of the most difficult process, I heard God tell me: "Today you do not understand your pain, but one day you will have many women before you. You will know their pain. And you will have My word in your mouth to comfort them and restore their lives."

At first, those words made no sense. How could I comfort myself if I myself was broken? Time and God's faithfulness showed me that everything I lived through was just preparation. Today, when I stand before women with stories of betrayal, loss, illness, or despair, I know I am not speaking from theory. I speak from the heaven that touched me. And now that same heaven is touching their lives.

What Heaven Can Do... and Will Continue to Do

> *"I will tell of all your wonders." (Psalm 9:1)*

This is just part of what God has done in me. Every word is a scar turned into testimony. His hand collected every tear.

Today I have life, purpose, family, and calling, because heaven intervened. There is nothing that heaven cannot transform. What seems impossible to you today is God's opportunity to show you His glory. He is a specialist in what no longer has a solution.

Conclusion: Heaven Can Also Touch Your Life

"I will proclaim all your marvelous deeds." (Psalm 9:1)

I am living evidence of what heaven can do. And if He did it with me, He can do it with you. Perhaps you do not understand your pain today, but God is already writing a story of redemption. Open your heart, and let heaven work. Because what heaven can do... has no limits.

Learn more about Pastor Jeannett Toro

JEANETT TORO WAS BORN on December 22, 1969, in Brooklyn, New York, to Puerto Rican parents: Sixto Hernández Gerena and Carmen Lydia Rodríguez. She is the second of four siblings and grew up in Carolina, Puerto Rico, where she completed her studies at Parcelas Buenaventura, Dr. Facundo Bueso schools, and Julio Vizcarrondo High School. From a young age, she showed great dedication to her professional training. She specialized in barbering at the Dr. Carlos F. Daniels vocational school and later graduated from the Puerto Rico Barber College as a barber, cosmetologist, and trichologist. For a time, she also worked as a cosmetology teacher. Later, she complemented her preparation with certifications as an esthetician at the Madison Institute and as a micropigmentation technician at the Micropigmentation Institute of Puerto Rico. With more than 25 years of business experience, Jeanett was the founder and owner of the successful salon "Extreme Jeany Salón," located near the Judicial Center of Carolina. After retiring as a beauty specialist, she continued to develop her creativity by excelling as a pastry chef and cake designer, recognized for her excellence and originality in every design. In June 1992, Jeanett married Rev. Neftalí Toro, with whom she has shared more than three decades of life and ministry. In 2012, the couple moved to the city of New Bedford, Massachusetts, responding to God's call to establish and found the Rebaño Casa de Adoración church, where they serve as lead pastors. That same year, they also started the Women's Ministry "In God We Will Do Exploits," a space for formation, fellowship, and spiritual strengthening for women. Within this ministry, Jeanett leads the project "A Coffee with the Pastor," a time of word, counseling, activities, and restoration that has blessed many women in the Kingdom and remains active to this day. Jeanett is the mother of two daughters: Pastor Neyshali Annette Toro-Lacén and worshiper Nayeli Athalia Toro. God has also blessed her home with her son-in-law, Pastor Derek Lacén. Her life is a living testimony to the power of heaven when a heart completely surrenders to the call of God.

Among Friends

FOURTEENTH STORY

THE WORSHIP

ESTER DELVILLAR
Dominican Republic

14

THE WORSHIP

BY ESTER DELVILLAR, SANTO DOMINGO

Many of us, at some point, have defined worship as a gentle song we sing in the congregation. Others, perhaps, have reduced it to a ministry through which people demonstrate their talent and ability to sing songs, delighting the listener.

However, when we look at the scenario in the Bible, in Genesis chapter 22, where worship is mentioned for the first time, we see something different. When the Lord asked Abraham to sacrifice his only son, Isaac, the promised son, we understand that worship is not about singing songs but about an act that encompasses two important things in the life of the believer:

1. Abraham offered God what he loved most.
2. Abraham obeyed God without questioning.

Another well-known event where we see the word worship is found in the Gospel of John 4:23, where the Lord has an encounter with a Samaritan woman. She had had several husbands, and the one she had at that moment did not belong to her either. The Lord engages in a conversation with her, seeking to reveal Himself to her life so that He would become her seventh and final "husband"—the one who fills everything in all. When we know Him, we reach the fullness of happiness. Intimacy with Him frees us from any other need.

In this scenario, we see once again that true worship is not about a song, a simple instrument, a stage, or a beautiful melody. It depends, primarily, on the attitude of a heart that has determined to draw near to the Lord with reality, conviction, humility, and simplicity. It is a heart that recognizes His power and majesty, that surrenders everything it has clung to in life, and that allows Jesus to govern its emotions, longings, and desires.

Worship is a continuous act of recognizing the Lord at all times: when we work, serve others, deal with others, in our daily lives, when we care for our family, and even in our most intimate struggles. It is living with the clear consciousness and conviction that we are the temple of His presence and that every action can become an act of surrender and honor to our God.

Sometimes we find ourselves in situations where it is urgent that we show the character of Jesus, and to achieve this, it is advisable to ask ourselves these questions: How would the Lord Jesus react in this situation? What would He answer in this conversation? What would He think? If we long to adopt His nature of love and holiness, then it is appropriate that we speak as He speaks, look as He looks, and act as He acts.

Worship is a lifestyle we can live for God. This includes the great challenge of submitting our emotions to His will and the self-control we must demonstrate in the face of the different situations we experience with our neighbor. Today, we live in a world corrupted to its fullest extent, and only by adopting the character of Jesus can we shine in the midst of so much darkness.

Proverbs 3:6 says:

> *"In all your ways submit to him, and he will make your paths straight."*

This means having a clear and constant awareness of who God is, being in communion with Him, and recognizing His presence in every aspect of our daily life, be it our actions, decisions, or plans. It means that by trusting in God and acknowledging Him, He will guide our steps and make our paths straight and safe.

My Experience

A while ago, I used to worship according to the circumstances, but when I learned to submit my longings and desires to the absolute will of God, choosing to cast my burdens upon Him, focusing only on who He is and the great sacrifice He made for the salvation of my soul, the intention of my worship and the way I approach Him changed.

Over the years, the Lord has been teaching me that the greater the surrender, the greater the glory that is manifested in our lives. No one can see the Lord's purpose fulfilled when we forget to involve Him in all our projects and desires, when we stop being humble and live with a heart attached to the earthly, chasing the vanity of life.

Throughout the years, I have seen how God has been shaping me in this recognition of who He is, what He deserves, and what I was created for. Therefore, without a doubt, I can express that to achieve a genuine level of worship, it is necessary to die to the self, die to wanting to be seen as the center, die to the pleasures of the world, to pride, to envy, to the desire to possess, and to the vanity of life. As we are broken and humbled, then Christ is lifted up.

I have learned that as we move away from what feeds our humanity, from everything that pleases the flesh, and choose to draw closer to Him, our heart becomes more sensitive to the touch of His Spirit. In this way, we can learn to hear His voice, feel His presence, and enjoy a beautiful relationship of friendship with the Father.

Importance of Intimacy with God

Intimacy is summarized in that willingness to be close to Him. It is so important because it strengthens our faith in the Lord in such a way that we can experience that peace that surpasses all understanding. The closer we get to Him, the more He reveals Himself to us and guides us at all times in this walk.

Intimacy with God is the result of a life of holiness, prayer, study of the word, and obedience. For this reason, I can say that congregational worship is only the reflection of what happens in personal worship. We cannot pretend to manifest the presence of God before others if we have not first cultivated a relationship of intimacy with Him. In that life of intimacy, without lights or applause, we surrender our will to Him. It is there that the character of the worshiper is formed, where we learn to depend on the Holy Spirit and not on our own talent. Jesus Himself left us the example. Before every miracle, before every public teaching, He sought a solitary place to be alone with the Father. If the Son of God had the need to create a relationship of intimacy with His Father, how much more must we live surrendered to Him!

An Uncontaminated Worship

James 4:8 teaches us:

> *"Come near to God and he will come near to you. Wash your hands, you sinners, and purify your hearts, you double-minded."*

The worshipper's heart must be clean. This means that we must maintain a spirit willing to be purified every day. Worship contaminated by pride, vanity, or the search for recognition loses its essence.

Ezekiel in his chapter 28 presents a picture of how arrogance and conceit can trigger someone's defeat. Knowing this, if we do not guard our hearts, we could find ourselves in a similar situation.

I mention this with the objective of making it clear that the worshiper was not established to be the center of attention, but to be the instrument that leads the people to the presence of God, exalting His majesty and giving due glory to His name.

The incense that went up in the tabernacle had to be pure so that it would be pleasing to God. In the same way, our worship must come from a willing, sincere, and humble heart.

The Worship That Transforms

Worship is not only an act of surrender but also of transformation. Every time we bow before God, He molds our character, heals our wounds, and clothes us with His presence. Worship changes us first, and then it affects those around us.

Worship transforms because, by focusing our attention on the character of God and surrendering our life to Him, we are molded from the inside out, becoming more like Him. This transformation fills us with joy, peace, gratitude, and drives us to live with new priorities and a purpose that honors our Creator in all areas of our lives.

I have lived moments when, without uttering a word, the presence of God has manifested with power. It was not because of what I could give, but because I had previously learned to surrender in secret. That is the key: what we do in the hidden is revealed in the public.

Conclusion

True worship is measured by the life we offer day after day. It is obeying when it is difficult, serving when no one applauds, forgiving when it hurts, and remaining faithful even in the midst of trials.

May our worship never depend on a visible altar, but spring from the invisible altar we carry in our hearts.

Learn more about Ester Delvillar

Ester Delvillar was born on February 25, 1988, in the city of Higüey, La Altagracia province, Dominican Republic, into an evangelical Christian home. From a very young age, she was instructed in the faith, developing a deep spiritual conviction that would mark the course of her life. Raised in a Christian environment where biblical principles were the foundation of her family upbringing, Ester grew up with a genuine love for God and for service in the church. Over the years, Ester consolidated her academic preparation, obtaining a Bachelor's Degree in Accounting and later a Bachelor's Degree in Theology, which reflects her passion for both the professional field and the study of the Word of God. Additionally, she is fluent in English as a second language, which has allowed her to navigate broader multicultural and ministerial contexts. Personally, Ester is married to Claubian Etius and is the mother of three children: two girls and one boy. Her family constitutes an essential part of her ministry, being an example of dedication, faith, and Christian love. As a homemaker, wife, and mother, she has been able to maturely balance her family responsibilities with her ministerial calling. Her trajectory within the church has been characterized by a heart sensitive to worship. Ester is recognized as a worshiper and worship leader, transmitting with her voice and her dedication a message of faith and hope that impacts lives. She has also been invited to share the Word as a preacher, imparting messages based on Scripture that edify and motivate spiritual growth. Ester Delvillar Arache is an upright, prepared, and committed woman who continues to develop her ministry with the firm purpose of glorifying God and being an instrument of blessing for present and future generations.

**ALFAXAD SÁNCHEZ
BRIDGEWATER, MA**

FIFTEENTH STORY

HEALING WITH FAITH

MENTAL HEALTH, A PROCESS OF VICTORIES IN CHRIST JESUS

HEALING WITH FAITH
"MENTAL HEALTH, A PROCESS OF VICTORIES IN CHRIST JESUS"

BY ALFAXAD SÁNCHEZ, BRIDGEWATER, MA

May God bless you greatly! My name is Alfaxad Sánchez, although I am better known as Merary Sánchez. I would like to share a little of my story, how I have faced mental health challenges. I do this as a call to awareness and hope for all those going through similar or difficult struggles.

Like any human being, I have had my ups and downs. Among those challenges, mental health has been one of the biggest. Through them, God has taught me about resilience, the importance of faith, and the value of community. I do not write these words to focus on pain or difficulties, but to share a process of growth, learning, and hope.

For years, I have struggled with mental health challenges, and I have had to learn to know myself better. I have experienced relapses that have made me reflect on the importance of mental health, self-care, the value of seeking support, talking to someone when we need it, and following professional recommendations.

These actions make a big difference in daily life. Far from defining me as a weak person, these experiences have strengthened me. Today I understand that every step, even the most difficult ones, was part of a path that led me to a greater awareness of myself and what it means to live fully, even after overcoming mental health challenges.

Discipline and Personal Growth

One of the most important learnings from this process is understanding that, just like physical health, mental health requires discipline and consistency to achieve a balanced life. It is not just about taking medication or attending a medical appointment, but about cultivating healthy habits: respecting sleep hours, eating properly, maintaining an exercise routine, and, above all, learning to listen to the body and mind when they alert us that something is wrong.

Today I understand that identifying triggers is one of the most valuable tools. Recognizing when I feel most vulnerable, learning to stop before falling into a crisis, and knowing who to turn to in those moments has been essential to maintaining balance. Each person has a different path, but something we all share is the need to observe ourselves, know ourselves, and respect our own processes.

The Value of Family and Community

In this journey, I also discovered that I do not walk alone. My family has been integral to my healing and hope. They, too, have learned with me; they have understood that mental health does not only affect the person diagnosed but also those who love and accompany them.

I have seen how a mother's love, the patience and tenderness of children, and the support of siblings and nephews can become firm pillars in the midst of challenges. When the family educates and organizes itself, it is capable of offering not only companionship but also motivation, structure, and a safe space where one feels understood.

That is why I always say mental health care is a team effort. The family also needs support, education, and spaces to better understand what it means to accompany someone with a mental health diagnosis. They deserve recognition, because their role is as fundamental as that of the patient themselves.

Faith, Science, and Psychoeducation

My faith has been another indispensable pillar. Being a daughter of God reminds me every day that I do not walk alone, that every battle brings with it a teaching, and that divine grace sustains me even in the most challenging moments.

Sometimes, in church contexts, those going through mental health conditions are judged, labeled, or misunderstood. I want to invite faith communities to look with different eyes: mental health is not a punishment or a lack of faith. It is part of our humanity, and attending to it is also honoring the body and mind that God gave us.

I believe prayer and faith complement medicine and therapy. For me, both have been paths to healing. God works through professionals, through treatments, through the scientific tools we have today, and He also works in the community around us.

Many times God reminds us of what His word says:

> *"My grace is sufficient for you, for my power is made perfect in weakness."* (2 Corinthians 12:9)

I write these lines as a call to promote mental health and break the stigmas that still exist. For a long time, ignorance led to people being labeled as "weak," "incapable," or even "demon-possessed." These words not only hurt but push away those who most need support.

That is why I deeply believe in psychoeducation. Educating oneself is an act of love. When we understand what a diagnosis means, how symptoms present, what treatments exist, and how we can help, we stop judging and start accompanying. Education opens the doors to understanding and closes the doors to discrimination.

Beyond the family and the church, the community as a whole plays a fundamental role. A neighbor who listens without judging, a teacher who understands, a co-worker who respects processes—all of them are part of that support network that strengthens and gives hope.

I have learned that mental health is built in the everyday: in a sincere conversation, in a hug, in a word of encouragement. When, as a society, we unite to care for those facing these struggles, we create an environment where healing is possible and where hope flourishes.

My life has not been perfect, but I have learned to see every experience as part of a process. The mental health diagnosis does not define me; what defines me is the way I respond, the way I learn from every fall, and the ability to get up with more strength and awareness.

Today I can say that every relapse has taught me something new: the importance of discipline, the humility to ask for help, and that I am not alone. Furthermore, it has given me the opportunity to serve others by sharing what I have learned. A mental health diagnosis has not been the end, but the beginning of a more conscious life, with purpose, more supportive, and committed.

I want to end this reflection with a sincere call:

- To those living with a mental health diagnosis: Do not give up. Your life has value, your struggles do not define you, and there is always a new dawn.
- To family members: Thank you for being there, for sustaining, for accompanying. Your love transforms and is an essential part of the path to healing.
- To the churches: Be a refuge, not a judge. Faith and mental health can walk hand in hand.
- To the entire community: Let's educate ourselves, support each other, let's break down the stigma.

Today I am still standing, not because I never fell, but because I learned that falling is part of the path, and love, hope, and faith are always stronger.

> *"But those who hope in the Lord will renew their strength. They will soar on wings like eagles; they will run and not grow weary, they will walk and not be faint." (Isaiah 40:31)*

Learn more about Alfaxad M. Sánchez

ALFAXAD M. SÁNCHEZ, better known as Merary Sánchez, was born in the Dominican Republic, a land that saw her grow up and that profoundly marked her roots and values. At age 22, she emigrated to Puerto Rico, where she began her university studies at the University of the Sacred Heart, focusing on Business Administration and Accounting. In 1997, Merary moved to Boston, Massachusetts, a city that became her second home and where she has developed a large part of her personal, academic, and professional life. There, she completed two associate degrees in Business Administration and Accounting at Roxbury Community College, laying the foundation for her first steps in the professional field. Over time, her vocation took a new direction toward the field of psychology and mental health. In 2020, she obtained her bachelor's degree in Psychology from the University of Massachusetts, Boston, an achievement that marked the beginning of a path of purpose and commitment to the well-being of others. Merary is currently pursuing a master's degree in Mental Health Counseling and Psychology at Framingham State University, with the firm goal of graduating in December 2025. Beyond academic achievements, her greatest blessing is being the mother of two precious children, whom she considers divine gifts and the engine of her dreams. They have been her inspiration to persevere and demonstrate that with effort, faith, and dedication, everything is possible. For the last 12 years, she has worked and served the community with passion and dedication, accompanying families and individuals in processes of personal improvement, emotional well-being, and strengthening bonds. Her work experience and academic preparation are intertwined with her genuine desire to provide hope, guidance, and practical tools to those facing challenges in their daily lives. Today, Merary Sánchez defines herself as a resilient, hardworking woman deeply committed to her faith and her community. Her story is a testimony of perseverance and transformation. Her goal is to continue developing as a mental health professional, with the vision of providing support to those who need it, especially in the Hispanic community, breaking down stigmas and promoting a full and healthy life.

Among Friends

SIXTEENTH
STORY

Honoring My Mother

Marisol Severino
Dominican Republic

16

HONORING MY MOTHER
BY MARISOL MARTÍNEZ, REPÚBLICA DOMINICANA

Before writing anything about myself, Marisol Martínez, I must honor my progenitor, my life mentor, my inseparable friend, Francisca Martínez y Cancú. She was born in Sánchez Samaná, Dominican Republic, on September 18, 1934 (she would have turned 91). Her legacy continues; as long as I live, I will honor her in the powerful name of our Lord and Savior Jesus Christ.

She instructed me in the ways of the Lord, as His word says; and as long as I live, I will not stop mentioning her for her great work and her mission with me, until her last breath.

I share that my mother had a serious complication at the time of my birth; both of us were going to die. We were rushed by emergency from my town, Sánchez, to the main provincial hospital in Samaná. I was the only one in my house born in Samaná, due to the seriousness we experienced, my mother and I, in her womb. But... God had a plan to execute in my life, and He used that wonderful, God-fearing being whom He loved as an instrument. She was an avid reader and connoisseur of the Holy Scriptures and, above all, she taught me with her life what it meant to live for God.

I learned to read and write with the Bible. We didn't have other books, nor could we buy them, but we did have the Bible. My mother was the superintendent of the local church's Sunday School for decades. I didn't study with books; we didn't have resources. In college, it was the first time I bought the basic books for my degree; everything else was copies or going to the library. But I will tell my memories on another occasion, because I want to express how grateful I am to the Father, Son, and Holy Spirit for having a mother like the one my siblings and I had; whom we describe as: a woman of unbreakable faith, with ethical principles and values, loving, counselor, selfless, protective, tireless fighter, optimistic, cheerful, resilient, an all-terrain, five-star mother. We will always remember you with love, we will love you forever.

Beloved readers, allow me to share some of the life experiences with her so you can get to know her a little.

I remember an elderly man in my community, who supposedly had no family or anyone near our house, whom my mother cleaned every day, brought food to, and washed his clothes, as he could not go to the bathroom. She medicated him; you understand the mission to be carried out with this elderly man, whom we learned to love and serve. I never heard my mom complain or say anything derogatory about the old man; she did it with so much love. I remember her boiling his clothes over a wood fire after washing them. My siblings and I joined the mission; we had to help Mom. This marked my life to the point that I remember even the old man's name; we called him Tima.

Another thing that marked me is that we lived near the church all our lives. Our house is on Duarte Street and the church on Sánchez Street; if you visit my town, you can confirm it. And we had to do everything in the church. I mean, from cleaning the latrine (for those who have known what a latrine is, which today is called a toilet or bathroom) to the hospitality of all the visitors invited by our pastors on duty. That is, I grew up serving in the Kingdom and for the saints of the Lord. We felt fortunate for this special mission of service; that's how she taught us.

I also remember that, before building the temple, when I was very young, the church decided to buy the pastor a house near the church, because he had to travel every day from the countryside to the town and most of the time on foot, at least the return trip. And the services ended when the Holy Spirit indicated it.

What I want to point out is that today my town has a temple that was the first, and I believe the only one in the council I belong to, that has a baptistery and that we have had radio and television programs in the temple. And I remember how hard we worked in my house to achieve it. Mom did not ask for any of her seven children, but to build a house for Jehovah, she asked and asked, to the point of letting me participate in several pageants and for her girl to travel to other towns to raise funds to make a dignified house for our God. We were in a totally dilapidated wooden shack. My mom requested help from the mayor's office, from businesses, and from everyone I can remember. She asked them, but Father God helped us to be part of the things of His Kingdom.

Since I can remember, I have served the Lord, glory to God for this! I am privileged, blessed. What an honor the Lord has granted me! I want to finish my race toward eternity with joy.

I cannot forget those moments of the family altar. It was non-negotiable; there was always that time of intimacy with God, the morning devotionals. I remember that she would put us to bed afterwards to go to school. She always recommended that we seek the Lord in the morning and would wake us up with those songs: *"I will seek the Lord in the morning"* and another one I remember is: *"In the morning in prayer, my God speaks to my heart."* She taught us how to lead a service, how she worshiped with such devotion and surrender. I loved to hear her sing; I learned to do it through her teachings. She always advised us not to grieve the Holy Spirit and respect the pulpit.

My mom was generous, giving, and very compassionate. At home, she didn't just cook for us; she always had someone in mind to feed. As we had property at that time, during harvests, she would make a list to set aside their provisions before selling them. She would slaughter an animal and share it with her neighbors, as was her custom.

On the other hand, when she could no longer attend church due to physical health issues, I remember that list with an envelope she sent with us, with tithes, offerings, first fruits, for the ladies, for the Dorcas club. It was an endless list of all the ministries in the church; she cooperated with everyone. Incredible, but very true and worth remembering. She always told us: *"Do not let your left hand know what your right hand is doing."* Do I have reasons to talk about my mother or not?

When my mom gave me the last life guidelines and had me write them down, I was impacted when she told me this (it makes me cry every time I remember): *"I know that you will not change, that you will continue with that sensitive heart you have, my daughter."* Those words echo in my mind, and I only ask my God to always honor Him, to love Him with all that I am. She fulfilled her mission with me. What a mother my siblings and I had!

There was a coincidence or God's purpose, as our Father always does what He wants with His children. That afternoon, specifically Thursday, September 7, 2023, my husband picked me up from work, and we went to visit a pastor friend who was already bedridden with a degenerative disease, which kept him disabled from taking care of himself. The Lord had touched us to help, as much as possible, not with much, but something. At the same time, my siblings were taking my mom to her regular cardiologist because she was not feeling well and asked to be taken. But first, she asked for a nurse who always assisted her and whom we consider part of my family, another daughter. And she says: *"It's strange that she hasn't visited me these days, since I've been feeling so bad."* My siblings informed her that the nurse had just had surgery, and she didn't want my mom to know. Well, my mom, with her medical emergency, asked to be taken to visit her before going to the clinic. She visited her and carried out her last mission: she prayed with her, who is now motherless. And they took her to the cardiologist. My mom and I were visiting the sick at the same time. But the commendable thing about this was that my mom was living her last hours of life and had a medical emergency: she was having minor heart attacks. Two or three hours later, she suffered a massive heart attack and departed in the presence of her Heavenly Father.

She died doing what I always saw her do: practicing life in Christ as His follower, not with words, but with deeds.

My mom grew up with a very good stepmother. That was the grandmother my siblings and I knew. Her mother died when she was a child. There was once an earthquake in my town, and the little house fell on her, small as she was, and the Lord brought her out alive to fulfill His purposes in her. My entire town witnessed my mom's rescue.

When I returned to the country from my vacation on Tuesday, January 10, 2023, I called Mom to tell her that we had arrived safely. We would just leave the suitcases at home to go see her. Ten days had already passed into this new year, and I was urgent to see her. She told me to leave it for Thursday, January 12, because she had an appointment in San Francisco de Macorís, at the Hospital Siglo XXI.

On Thursday, January 12, 2023, sitting together, just the two of us as always, she told me: *"Do you know where I am going, my daughter?"*, and she didn't continue speaking until I answered her. I told her yes, I said: *"Oh, Mom, let's not start this year like this, don't do this to me!"*, and I started crying. She said: *"See why I tell you, don't cry, be strong, sing my hymns to me...". "I won't be able to,"* I said, *"don't make me promise, you know how I am." "Remember what I always tell you: protect yourselves, love each other, take care of each other as siblings and family,"* she repeated the same thing to me: *"If each of you has something, you unite and don't suffer hardship. Don't harm anyone, give a plate of food even to your enemies, and serve people. Mari, it is for your own good to love, forgive, serve."* My mom was trying to prepare me for her departure. She did not succeed; I feel empty without her, with deep sadness. Nothing replaces her wise and timely advice, her unconditional love, and her presence. That's how I think, and that's how I feel until today.

Mom marked us in everything she did. She was a resilient warrior. She shared her essence with us, the love for God with her mind, with her heart, with all her strength. Her dedication, surrender, and tireless service for the work in the body of our Lord and Savior Jesus Christ, His church, in whatever position she was appointed to. She was relevant; she understood that she was only a collaborator in the Kingdom of God, that it is our God who produces in us both the will and the deed (Philippians 2:13).

Until her final days, she said everything she did was for His glory. And we all, as a family, can attest to that.

Even in the last hours of her life, on the afternoon of Thursday, September 7, she made her last visit (she couldn't), but as the Holy Scriptures say:

> *"Religion that God our Father accepts as pure and faultless is this: to look after orphans and widows in their distress and to keep oneself from being polluted by the world." (James 1:27)*

For over five decades, my mom suffered from chronic asthma. This triggered other catastrophic illnesses in her, such as an enlarged and slow heart. She never complained; I remember as a child that when those crises hit, she would only tell us: "Pray, don't cry." She taught us that prayer and worship are weapons of mass destruction against evil in our lives.

No matter the situation you are going through, the arid desert, those hard and bitter moments of constant processes, where you don't see the light at the end of the tunnel, where everyone has abandoned, despised, and ignored you, my Father, your Father, has a plan for you. He improvises nothing; He is perfect and always arrives on time. Seek Him, always ask Him for everything without reservation, and do not hold anything back. He is attentive to you, He is detail-oriented, He never neglects His role, He is never too busy to attend to us. Conquer your intimacy with Him; there is nothing like being intimate with Him—you feel protected, pampered, loved, and never ignored. I present to you Almighty God, who loves you. Accept His eternal love today.

Learn more about Marisol Martínez S.

MARISOL CELESTE MARTÍNEZ de Severino is a native of Sánchez, Samaná, Dominican Republic. She is the youngest of the women in a family of seven siblings, followed only by her male brothers. She has served God since she was old enough to know right from wrong, a lifelong privilege for which she is grateful; she was baptized in water at approximately 11 years of age. In her academic training, she completed her primary studies at the Pablo Pumarol School, and her secondary studies at the Academia Duarte College. She pursued her university studies at the Universidad Dominicana O&M, where she was part of the first group of seven licensed graduates in Secretarial Sciences in her country. She has complemented her education with numerous extracurricular courses, including Television Production at the National School of Scenic Art, Film, TV, Inc., and she is a Professional Announcer, having studied at the Esdras School of Announcing. She has been married for over 40 years to Lic. Marcos Severino, and they have one son, Arq. Marcos Severino Martínez. At the ecclesiastical level, and by the grace of God, Marisol has held various positions in her council in the Dominican Republic. She was National Director of Youth, National Director of Communications, National

Director of Public Relations, and National Secretary of the Council Office. In addition, she was the host and producer of the television program Visión Ahora, the first live program produced by Dominicans on state television, and the radio program Bloque Radial de la Profecía (Prophecy Radio Block) on Radio Ven la Voz Evangélica Nacional. Currently, she is the CEO of the Radio and Television Program Conectados con Dios (Connected with God) since 2015 in Boston, with an extension in Santo Domingo. She and her family served as pastors for six years and six months in Worcester, MA, during the period 2009-2015, which was a great honor. In her theological training, she has completed studies at the Gordon-Conwell Theological Seminary (currently in progress), in addition to other studies completed in the Church of God of Prophecy council, to which she belongs, specifically in its institutes, such as the Bible Training Institute (IEB) and the Biblical Leadership Center (CLB).

SEVENTEENTH
STORY

THE VALUE OF THE PROCESS IN HUMAN AND SPIRITUAL LIFE

Sheila Dávila
New Bedford, MA

17

THE VALUE OF THE PROCESS IN HUMAN AND SPIRITUAL LIFE

PASTOR SHEILA DÁVILA, NB, MA

How Suffering, Trials, and Perseverance Strengthen Faith, Character, and Hope in God

Everything in life speaks to us of process, including the cycle of human life: infancy, adolescence, youth, adulthood, and old age.

Nature also follows processes, like that of a plant (which takes about 21 days, depending on the environment): planting, germination, growth, reproduction, respiration, and photosynthesis. After its process, comes flowering, fruit development, and ripening. The process of the butterfly, or metamorphosis (which takes from 21 days to 1 month), includes the egg, the larva, the chrysalis, and finally, the butterfly. Before spreading its wings and achieving flight, there is a process.

All this demonstrates that we cannot avoid, interrupt, or interfere with the process. Our entire process has a beginning, a time, a purpose, and an end that is not forever. It brings growth, maturation, production, development, flowering, and flight.

When Does the Process Arrive in Our Life?

Job asked: "Why then did you bring me out of the womb?" (Job 10:18). In the midst of his process and suffering, he inquired why God had caused him to be born to experience so much pain, preferring not to have existed. He was a God-fearing man, but the process was severe and painful. He lost his possessions, his children, and illness arrived. To top it all off, his three friends, Teman, Bildad, and Eliphaz, acted as judges and lawyers instead of comforting him.

My personal process began in 2009. One morning I woke up unable to move, comb my hair, or wash my mouth by myself. I was unable to care for myself for 15 days. At the hospital, despite multiple labs, there was no clinical explanation. Three months later, I woke up with a swollen mouth and unable to speak well. I was sent to an emergency ENT specialist, as my mouth and tongue were swollen, sore, bleeding, and oozing pus. Biopsies and cultures were performed, but the results continued to come back "fine." The doctors began to suggest that everything was caused by anxiety, depression, and stress.

Three months later, I awoke worse. The swelling had affected my eyes. I saw several specialists (generalists, infectiologists, cardiologists, rheumatologists, neurologists, gynecologists, ophthalmologists, allergists), and all the tests kept coming back fine. I began to feel frustrated, like Job, for not understanding the reason for that suffering. My faith was drowning, and I felt like I was swimming with only one lung. Every new flare-up was more severe. Then, the condition began to affect intimate parts of my body. I couldn't urinate; my intimate area was swollen, raw, bleeding, and oozing pus, which forced me to urinate in cold water and with anesthesia. I also couldn't eat or speak, and could only swallow water slowly, using anesthesia in my mouth, to hydrate myself.

I knew what Romans 8:28 said, "All things work together for good to those who love God," and Psalm 23:4, "Even though I walk through the valley of the shadow of death, I will fear no evil, for you are with me," and that my help "comes from the Lord" (Psalm 121).

However, it was difficult for me to look up to heaven. Knowing the Word did not prevent my roller coaster of emotions, feelings, and thoughts. On my wedding day (11/19/2011), I could not eat the cake, nor could I have a honeymoon, as the doctor had to inject me early so that the photos would turn out as well as possible.

I went to the Cave of Adullam like David, with my loneliness, affliction, pain, and frustration. I asked for the wings that David asked for to fly away like a dove (Psalm 55:6), wishing to escape that stormy wind and flee to the desert. I felt that the waters entered my soul (Psalm 69), sinking into a miry bog, where the current overwhelmed me. I was weary of crying out; my throat was hoarse, and my eyes failed from waiting for my God.

God Had a Purpose

I remember one morning when I bowed down to pray, and my tears were my prayer. I heard a song that said: "Draw near to the Lord with gratitude... and lift up your voice with joy." He asked me to give thanks and worship in the darkest moment. I sang it mentally, shouting it with effort so that my tears would not fall near my mouth. The Holy Spirit interceded for me with groans too deep for words (Romans 8:26).

The Holy Spirit Helps Us

In our weakness, when we cannot verbalize anything or make any sound, He takes our place and expresses to the Father what we need. The Holy Spirit is our Paraclete, Comforter, help, Counselor, Defender, and Intercessor.

In my process, the "Teman, Bildad, or Eliphaz" (Job's friends) were not lacking, nor was the religious person who said: "You have to pray more, fast more, and trust more." But in my process, God never failed me. His Word was my refuge, sustenance, anchor, and security. The church, their love, their prayer, their care, and support were important; my pastors Carmen Rivera and José Rosa never let go of me.

After several years, they finally came up with my clinical diagnosis: the autoimmune disorder disease, Behcet's Disease. This condition causes vasculitis, inflammation of the blood vessels, nervous system problems, blurred vision, chronic pain, clots, inflammation of the brain and spinal cord, and can cause blindness and disability. Upon hearing this, the doctor told me: "Mrs. Dávila, I am very sorry, but there is no cure for this disease. There is only treatment: anti-inflammatories, immunosuppressants, intravenous infusion, prednisone, and medications to suppress the immune system."

Faced with such a devastating diagnosis, anxiety, depression, and panic attacks began to develop. For a time, I was treated for anxiety until a verse found me: Proverbs 18:14:

> *"The spirit of a man will sustain his sickness, but a wounded spirit who can bear?"*

One day, in the supermarket parking lot, the symptoms began: I swelled up quickly, and my mouth started to burn. I quickly took out the powder and lip gloss, looked in the mirror, and said: "No more discouragement. I can do all things through Christ who strengthens me" (Philippians 4:13).

Courage is Crucial in the Face of a Chronic Condition

I cried, I put on a little makeup, I took a photo, I made an effort, and I smiled at the mirror. I said to myself: "Learn to live with the best attitude in the world." The Word was my cheerleader at all times. Proverbs 17:22 says: "A cheerful heart is good medicine, but a crushed spirit dries up the bones." Part of healing is having a good spirit. Courage is medicine; sometimes, part of the cure and relief is within ourselves, not outside.

God said I would be a pastor, and I wondered: "How?" But I embraced faith, strengthened hope, worked on my spirit, and faced that giant called disease. It was not with sword or with army, but with His Holy Spirit. I came to know God as never before: I knew Him as my Rapha ("Healer"), my Shalom ("Peace"), my Roi ("The One who sees me"), my Adonai ("My Lord"), my Abba Father ("daddy, papa, dad"). I felt His great paternal love.

The process brought me closer to Him, I knew Him deeply, and it led me not to abandon my faith, my character, or my fidelity and leadership. Three things are tested in the process: Faith, Character, and Fidelity.

Shepherd your soul in the process. Psalm 103 exhorts us: "Bless the Lord, O my soul, and all that is within me, bless His holy name. Bless the Lord, O my soul, and forget not all His benefits." I struggled to remind my soul not to forget any of His favors, mercies, and rescues. Psalm 42:5 asks: "Why are you cast down, O my soul, and why are you disquieted within me? Hope in God." It invites your soul to wait and praise.

The Word is the sustenance:

- It helps you manage emotions
- It maintains balance
- It provides faith, hope, and comfort
- It rescues life from the pit
- It takes our feet out of the miry pit and mud of despair.

If you patiently wait for the Lord in the process, He will set your feet upon a rock and give you a new song. Give yourself permission to cry, scream, feel bad, and ask questions. Do not suppress what you feel; take it to the cross and talk with Dad. God will not stop loving you because of how you feel, nor will He change the opinion He has of you. Don't pressure yourself; take one day at a time.

I Pleaded Like Paul

I pleaded that this thorn be taken away. I did not plead three times; I pleaded a hundred times, and the Lord told me in 2 Corinthians 12:9:

> *"My grace is sufficient for you, for my power is made perfect in weakness."*

I felt like Paul on his fourth journey to Rome (Acts 27), when the sun, moon, and stars were hidden. I felt adrift; the compass of my boat broke. I thought I would lose my life, but I continued to trust in the midst of that storm of illness. The angel of the Lord told Paul: "You will not lose your life. It is necessary." Without process and events, there would have been no outcome. What would Paul have written about in his 13 letters, what was he going to counsel or testify about? The apostle who achieved the greatest geographical reach had to suffer much.

Paul's process (2 Corinthians 11:24-28) included beatings, shipwrecks, dangers from robbers, hunger, cold, and, in addition to everything, the concern for all the churches.

The process seems to be taking away from you, but God is giving you. It seems like you are losing, but you are winning. It seems like God is subtracting from you, but He is adding to you. It seems like you are losing your life, but He is shaping you. There is no growth without process; there is no learning without process. Without weakness, there is no perfection.

You can feel like the plant or the butterfly, but God is going to be glorified. It is a matter of trusting, waiting, giving thanks, resisting, and not fainting.

Daniel's process included captivity, being accused of treason, and being thrown into the lions' den. The result was that he became governor of the province of Babylon and Minister of the king, maintaining his faith, righteousness, and integrity. Joseph's process included being rejected, mocked, imprisoned, and thrown into a cistern. The result was that he became second in command of Egypt, saved his family from famine, and was vested with the highest authority.

Keep going in your process. Do not give up, do not faint. Today, by His grace and favor, my husband and I pastor a beautiful congregation in New Bedford, Massachusetts, that was a witness and part of this process. God fulfilled His promises. If you remain faithful and firm, He will fulfill yours. He did it with me, with Paul, Daniel, Joseph, and Job. He will do it. Without my process, I also would not have been able to write my story to you. May His Word be the rescue in the midst of your process.

Learn more about Sheila Dávila

THE PASTOR SERVES at the Church of God Restoration Ministry in New Bedford, MA. She has been married for 14 years and is a mother to four beautiful children. She has been serving the Lord for 17 years. Her background includes studies at the Bible Institute of the Church of God New England Region, in addition to participating in seminars on Mental Health and Christian Education. Before assuming the pastorship, she performed various roles within the local church ministry, such as cleaning leader, Bible school teacher, deacon, and church counselor. For many years, she was the main support for her pastors. She expresses deep gratitude to her pastors, Bishop José A. Rosa and Pastor Carmen L. Rivera, for their support, help, teachings, and care, and, above all, for believing in her ministry. She considers them a school of formation and a fundamental example in her life. She has a great passion for reading and teaching the Word of the Lord. She is enthusiastic about visiting hospitals, visiting the elderly, and providing services to homes. She finds nature to be her favorite place to relax. Since she was seven years old, her father received a prophetic word that has materialized today by having the privilege of pastoring. She comes from a family of six with a solid foundation in faith. She had an excellent childhood, was an athlete in Puerto Rico, a skating champion, and a professional model. In 2004, she moved to New Bedford, MA, where she currently resides.

EIGHTEENTH
STORY

LOIS AND EUNICE: AN EXAMPLE FOR THE GENERATIONS

María L. Callejas
Medellín, Colombia

LOIS AND EUNICE: AN EXAMPLE FOR THE GENERATIONS

PASTOR MARÍA LIGIA CALLEJAS, MEDELLÍN, COLOMBIA

The Apostle Paul writes to his "beloved son" (2 Timothy 1:2) in this letter, expressing his deep affection for the young Timothy and valuing the work done by his grandmother Lois and his mother Eunice, both Jewish. Paul states that they persevered in the doctrine of their ancestors, surely based on the principle of Deuteronomy 4:6-8 and 6:6-9, now joined with the faith attained through Jesus Christ.

The apostle makes an intentional reference to the religion and citizenship of Timothy's father, who was Greek (Acts 16:1), which implies that he was neither a believer nor converted (Acts 16:3b).

The work of these two women is admirable. With time, wisdom, instruction, love, patience, and determination, and against all odds, their effort bore fruit. Friends, if you sometimes see women only complaining, make the decision that this will no longer be your case.

The genuine and unwavering faith possessed by the mother and grandmother was the powerful influence Timothy received since his childhood. 2 Timothy 3:15 says:

"And how from infancy you have known the Holy Scriptures, which are able to make you wise for salvation through faith in Christ Jesus."

In this way, Timothy was prepared to know whom to open his heart to, and he did so to the Son of God, his Savior.

The apostle refers to the disciple as his "true child in the faith" (1 Timothy 1:2) and states that his faith was "genuine, unfeigned" (2 Timothy 1:5), a faith that first dwelt in his grandmother and his mother (2 Timothy 1:5b).

To dwell, in both Hebrew and Greek, implies to remain, stable and deep residence, to abide (1 Timothy 1:5). This is the faith that dwells and remains in the apostle Paul's beloved "son in the faith."

Now, the mentor has a prepared field in his hands and the task of training the future pastor of Ephesus in his spiritual and ministerial character. Paul and Timothy meet in Lystra, where the brothers of the church vouch for Timothy's testimony (Acts 16:1-2). The apostle, being the third influential person in the young man's life, wanted him to go with him and circumcised him (Acts 16:3).

Paul urges him (1 Timothy 4:12-16) to:

1. Be an example (v. 12).
2. Not allow the contempt of his youth (v. 12).
3. Exhort, teach, and read (v. 13), taking advantage of the fact that he was an excellent reader due to Jewish discipline.
4. Be occupied in these things (v. 15).
5. Prioritize His life and the doctrine (v. 16).

Furthermore, he advises him (2 Timothy 1:6-7) to: stir up the gift of God (v. 6), be courageous and have self-control (v. 7), and not be ashamed (v. 8).

Finally, the apostle seals this treatise on Timothy, his "beloved son" (2 Timothy 1:2), with this exhortation (2 Timothy 3:14-15): "But as for you, continue in what you have learned and have become convinced of, because you know those from whom you learned it, and how from infancy you have known the Holy Scriptures, which are able to make you wise for salvation through faith in Christ Jesus."

Timothy is the result of a developed faith that transcends at home, in the warmth of a home that was not perfect, for it is in crises and conflicts where faith grows, is strengthened, seeks solutions, and resolves.

An Inspiring Testimony

Elvira, a mother from Antioch, Colombia, also serves as an inspiration. She had twelve children, three natural miscarriages, and two deceased children, totaling seventeen pregnancies. In her Catholic faith, she always begged the Lord with the deep desire to have a son who would be a priest. Later, she converted to the Lord, and her petition changed to God granting her a son who would be a pastor. God answered her, allowing her to see, before she died, four sons as pastors, thus multiplying her request. A large part of her family—children, grandchildren, and great-grandchildren—walk with Christ today.

Reflection and Call

Dear friend, this beautiful picture of faith should encourage you to make decisions and grow in your life as a believer.

Do you realize the powerful influence that God wants you to be? How much can we as women of faith contribute to our future generations? What concept do our children and grandchildren have of us as women of God?

You and I can, with God's help, change our world and that of our loved ones.

Come, pray with me for that heritage and fruit of your womb, with Psalm 127:3-5:

> "Behold, children are a heritage from the Lord, the fruit of the womb is a reward. Like arrows in the hand of a warrior, so are the children of one's youth. Happy is the man who has his quiver full of them; They shall not be ashamed when they speak with their enemies in the gate."

With affection, Your friend, María Ligia Callejas de T.

Learn more about María Ligia Callejas

BORN IN MEDELLÍN, Colombia, María Ligia is a woman of firm faith, a generous heart, and a helpful spirit. She describes herself as a loving, empathetic, and dedicated person, with a strong temperament that she has learned to put at the service of love and truth. She has been married for 45 years to Carlos Arturo Torres Arango and is the mother of three children—one son and two daughters—whom she considers her greatest blessing and testimony of God's faithfulness. For 38 years, she has served as a Christian Minister in the FCB (AD), carrying a message of hope and restoration through teaching and spiritual accompaniment.

In her academic training, she is a Theologian from the Biblical Seminary of the Assemblies of God in Colombia, a Nursing Assistant from SENA (National Learning Service), and a High School Graduate from the Carmelita Arcila School in Medellín, Colombia. Her pastoral vocation and her training in the health field have allowed her to integrate faith and service from a deeply human perspective.

Additionally, she completed the Diploma in Family Conciliation at the Pontifical Bolivarian University (UPB) in Medellín and obtained the Certificate in Mental Health and Addictions at the Interamerican University of Puerto Rico. She also strengthened her call to service through studies in Biblical Theology at the Biblical Seminary of Colombia. Throughout her life, María Ligia has been an example of dedication, prayer, and unconditional love, inspiring many women to believe that faith heals, sustains, and transforms.

Currently, she and her husband are focused on the development of the work through KOinonia Internacional, joining local churches, pastors, and work teams.

CONCLUSION

DON'T TIRE OF LOVING

Edna L Isaac
Taunton, MA

CONCLUSION
DO NOT TIRE OF LOVING

BY PASTOR EDNA L ISAAC

Beloved readers, we have reached the end of our book. My heart overflows with gratitude as I witness these powerful writings that have touched the deepest fibers of the soul. In every story and every account, one perceives the humility, sincerity, and heart of these exceptional co-authors, women who deserve all our respect and admiration. As I read each story, my eyes filled with tears, and my heart rejoiced in the presence of God upon hearing stories I had not heard before, stories of such impact that they touched my heart, and I know they would touch yours too. Truly, I have no words to thank God for each of these women who contributed their writing to this book. Each of these narratives, told from the soul, will not be forgotten but has been immortalized for the next generations. We thank each of them, and we hope, beloved reader, that upon reaching this page, your heart also overflows with gratitude for having had the opportunity to read them and to be touched by their truth.

Friendship in a World of Distrust

OUR CURRENT SOCIETY evidences a profound lack of true friends. We live in a world that constantly encourages fighting for one's own rights, discourages those who wish to love unconditionally, and mocks those who long for a love based on unconditional faithfulness. This type of affection has been labeled as obsolete, since the predominant narrative drives people to seek their own interests first.

We are even taught from a young age to "love ourselves first" and "not to let anyone take us for a fool," which inadvertently sows the seed of distrust. I remember being raised with the phrase that I later repeated to my children: "Don't trust anyone." While I agree with the need to be prudent and careful, that negative connotation has cost me many opportunities and has caused moments where I have sabotaged my own success due to that ingrained inability to trust.

We need to change this narrative and sow in the next generations love, trust, loyalty, and mutual respect. We need to set the example that Eunice and Lois exercised in Timothy's life; we need a generation full of love, not hate, full of peace, not chaos, full of empathy, not narcissists. We need to embody the Word that says in Proverbs 18:24: "A man who has friends must show himself friendly, and there is a friend who sticks closer than a brother."

I love staying positive and believing in opportunities, and I truly believe that real friends still exist. You can still trust. You can still love. Let's begin with a simple principle: we must show ourselves to be friendly if we genuinely want to have friends and cultivate meaningful relationships.

A Call for Genuine Connection

God designed human beings to live in friendship and harmony, and to share with others. Unfortunately, life experiences isolate us, and many times we prefer to stay on the sidelines, either due to distrust or having suffered betrayal, deception, or mistreatment.

However, today we make a call to you to draw near to someone and seek a true friendship. Remember that authentic friendship will suffer in different ways, but the important thing is to remain firm through thick and thin. God will sustain us at all times; He is our unwavering helper and comforter.

Do not grow tired of doing good. Do not grow tired of loving. Do not grow tired of giving opportunities. After all, imitate Jesus, who was a friend until the end, even when He spoke those words on the cross of Calvary: "Father, forgive them, for they do not know what they are doing."

Propose to love, even if that love is not reciprocated. Pray to God to keep people who will harm you away from you and, instead, bring you closer to friends who will help you grow in the Lord and make a difference.

The Love That Transcends the "Self"

As Marisol Martínez shared in her beautiful prologue "Beyond the 'SELF'," true friendship requires a redefinition. It is not just greeting each other occasionally on social media; it is something much deeper. Being a friend means being present when others leave. It is taking off your cloak and tunic and giving them away, even if you are left stripped. It is being present in the most painful moments and in the most exciting joys. It is loving selflessly and giving everything without expecting anything in return. The example of a supposed "friend" I had a long time ago, comes to mind. She was my "friend" as long as I gave her everything she asked for. I was the only one who always gave, the one who sacrificed herself and attended to all her requests, but nothing ever came from her side. I did it selflessly and with love because whenever I had a friendship, I gave myself completely, which is why I stopped having "friends." I was left with only one friend, Jesus. But with this supposed friend, I thought we got along very well. However, as soon as my finances changed and I had nothing even for myself, the friendship vanished; she simply disappeared. That is not being a friend. A friend does not demand, does not ask, does not insist. Quite the opposite: they are willing to give and to bless without expecting a reward, because they know that everything one does, they do as for God and not for men.

Let Us Love Like Jesus

Let us learn to love as Jesus did: He gave His life for His friends. May this book be a catalyst for your life to become an extension of His unconditional love. But above all, let us teach our children that we can still love and have compassion. Lets leave a legacy that transcends, let us leave a legacy that speaks more than a thousand words. Let us love from the heart, not self-interest. Let us love sacrificially, let us give without expecting anything in return. Let us give more than we receive and not hold it against others; in the long run, the reward comes from God. Let us give everything even if we are not given everything.

When the Apostle told the Church, especially the husbands, in verse 25 of chapter 5,

> *"Husbands, love your wives, just as Christ also loved the church and gave Himself up for her,"*

That is the way we must love, and not just our spouses. In other words, Christ knew that the Church would be unfaithful, ungrateful, ignorant on many occasions, cold, or careless, and contaminating itself with other idols, yet, even so, He gave Himself up for her.

If we loved this way, I'm sure things would be very different in the society we live in.

We hope this book has blessed your life, just as it has blessed us in writing it. If you wish to contact any of our co-authors or this servant, we want to hear from you; visit our websites or send an email to jdncpublications@gmail.com, and we will put you in direct contact with them. If you wish to bring the annual Entre Amigas (Among Friends) conference to your country or place where you live, write to us at entreamigasint@gmail.com.

Blessings.

Among Friends

ACKNOWLEDGMENTS

THANK YOU
THANK YOU
THANK YOU

ACKNOWLEDGEMENTS

Primarily, I want to give all the glory and honor to our Heavenly Father God, who is the source of all blessings, knowledge, and power. With all my heart, I thank every co-author who so lovingly accepted this challenge and dedicated their valuable time to fulfill this commitment.

Your stories and everything you shared made me cry, laugh, and rejoice as I saw how God is glorified in every account. Thank you for allowing the Lord to use you this way. I hope this is just the beginning of a writing career of excellence and edification. I wish you every success in your ministries, families, businesses, and personal lives. I cannot fail to mention you by name:

Alfaxad Sánchez, Claudia P. Álvarez, Dinora Puello, Dorothy Álvarez, Elizabeth Puello, Elizabeth Walcott, Erica V. Figueroa, Ester Delvillar, Gerianne Marra, Jeannett Toro, Jenny Fortes, Judith De la Espriella, Judian Bartolomey, Keren Sánchez, María Ligia Callejas, Marisol Martínez, Marisol Martínez S., Nilsa M. Ortiz, Sheila Dávila.

I truly admire you, I wish you much success in the Lord, and I hope this is neither the only nor the last project we work on together. You have a super wonderful potential that, in the hands of the Lord, will touch multitudes. All of you have the potential to be great writers who honor God with your writings. JND Publications and EDUCATE Publishing are here to help you reach that potential to its maximum power.

Blessings, my beloved ones,
Edna L Isaac

www.ingramcontent.com/pod-product-compliance
Lightning Source LLC
Chambersburg PA
CBHW061759070526
44586CB00023B/2629